THE

Little Women

COOKBOOK

Novel Takes on Classic Recipes
from Meg, Jo, Beth, Amy, and Friends

Jenne Bergstrom
- AND -
Miko Osada

Published by:
ULYSSES PRESS
PO Box 3440
Berkeley, CA 94703
www.ulyssespress.com

ISBN: 978-1-64604-540-2 (paperback)
ISBN: 978-1-61243-943-3 (hardback)
Library of Congress Control Number: 2019942070

Little Women illustrations and quotes are from the 1896 edition published by Little, Brown, and Company written by Louisa May Alcott with illustrations by Frank T. Merrill and Edmund H. Garrett.

Printed in Korea
10 9 8 7 6 5 4 3 2 1

Acquisitions editor: Casie Vogel
Managing editor: Claire Chun
Editor: Lauren Harrison
Proofreader: Kate St. Clair
Front cover and interior design: Malea Clark-Nicholson
Little Women illustrations from scans by the Internet Archive courtesy of the New York Public Library: pages 3, 4, 6, 12, 13, 16, 17, 20, 21, 28, 30, 31, 34, 38, 42, 51, 54, 55, 56, 60, 61, 66, 67, 68, 70, 76, 81, 82, 83, 86, 87, 88, 94, 97, 100, 101, 102, 110, 116, 123
Artwork from shutterstock.com: silhouettes © fresher; food and equipment icons © Kraphi and © Ku_suriuri; line ornaments © Roberto Castillo
Photographs from shutterstock.com: omelet © paulista; vegetables © VH-Studio; currant jam © Maslova Valentina; gingerbread © MShev; roast beef © Atsushi Hirao; peach pie © Tammy Veneziaa; seeded muffins © SMarina; sweet potatoes © MShev; hot lemonade © Sea Waves; roast chicken © Koliadzynska Iryna; lemon cake © Elisabeth Coelfen; charlotte russe © Nigina Sharipova; pink ice cream © joanna wnuk; loaf cake © Maria_Usp; potato rolls © cesarza; cale-cannon © Monkey Business Images; English muffins © P Kyriakosn; tea © Mybona

*This book is dedicated to our parents,
who raised us to be readers and eaters.*

Contents

PREFACE

If you've picked up this book, we're guessing that you've probably already read *Little Women,* or at least watched one of the many movie and TV adaptations. But in case you're a more casual visitor, here's a quick recap: The story follows four sisters, Meg, Jo, Beth, and Amy, who live in New England during the American Civil War era. Their father is away as a chaplain in the Union Army and their finances are not in great shape, but they do their best to enjoy life and improve themselves despite difficult times. Over the 10 years that the book covers, they grow from idealistic teenagers to mature adult women (with one sad exception). Even though many details of daily life have changed, the characters are so lovable and realistic that *Little Women* has been in print continuously for over 150 years! We both read our copies to pieces as children and teens, and we continue to find new things to enjoy in the story as adults.

We, the authors of this cookbook, are librarians by day and spend our free time making food and beverages from our favorite stories. Re-creating fictitious dishes is an immersive, 4D experience of our most beloved books. Especially in *Little Women,* where the novel centers on domestic life, the menus the characters choose and enjoy give us hints and insights about their personalities and priorities, and help us better understand them. Having a themed meal makes it that much easier to pretend we're in that era—we think of the food as an extra detail to cosplay! And so we asked the question: What exactly would the March sisters have eaten? After perusing hundreds of 19th-century recipes (or receipts, as they called them back then), we present you this book as our response to this worthy query.

of Puritans, liked meals of baked or stewed meat, boiled vegetables, and pie.1 But you're mistaken if you assume their food was all boring and bland. For one thing, Victorians made a vast array of their own condiments to season their food— curries, catsups, pickles, and gravies of all kinds. (We've included just a few samples in this book for you to try.) Plus, international cuisine already had a strong presence on the middle-class table in the 19th century. In the mid-1800s, advances in the railroad and canning industries allowed supplies to be sent quickly from one end of the country to the other, and even the most budget-conscious cookbooks required ingredients that had to be imported from all over the world: chocolate, coffee, tea, spices, citrus fruits, and tapioca, for example.2

A BITE-SIZED HISTORY

Let's start with a little history of Northern Civil War–era cuisine. New Englanders, as descendants

FOOD IS TRENDY

Going through old cookbooks makes you realize that food is as trendy as fashion. Dishes,

1   Helen Zoe Veit, *Food in the Civil War Era: The North* (East Lansing: Michigan State University Press, 2014), 14.
2   Veit, *Food in the Civil War Era: The North*, 31–32.

ingredients, and culinary methods that were popular in the 1800s might surprise or weird us out today, just as the idea of wearing a hoopskirt daily is decidedly unappealing to most modern readers. For example, we prefer to eat vegetables *al dente*, so to us, it seems like Victorians cooked theirs for a ridiculously long time. (They want us to boil the summer squash for 45 minutes!?) More differences between Americans then and now: Victorian bakers were reaching for their nutmeg where we would add vanilla, and nutmeg was also as common in savory dishes as pepper. We struggled to find a cookie recipe from the period, but there were endless options for blanc-manges and puddings. Finally, there are whole genres of cooking that aren't included in the typical American repertoire anymore. "Sweetmeats," for example, included preserved and candied fruits. And in most 19th-century cookbooks, there's a chapter devoted to "invalid cookery," or food for the sick, since medical care was usually administered at home.[3] (See Dainty Dishes starting on page 60 for more details!)

COOKING WAS A CHORE

Even for the most enthusiastic 21st-century chef, cooking can still feel like a chore sometimes. But imagine if you lived in the 1800s, when the whole process was a gigantic pain. First, you'd have to get the ingredients ready.... Wait, but there was no one-stop grocery store, so shopping meant visiting multiple shops. Food was only available according to season: fresh produce in summer and early autumn, shellfish in winter, and lamb in spring. (Take a look at *What Shall We Eat? A*

Manual for Housekeepers, an 1868 cookbook that suggests menus for every day of the year. It's fascinating!) Chicken is a standard dinner meat now, but back then, poultry was considered fancy because you had to take the extra step of plucking the feathers—you might have even bought it live from the butcher, so you'd have to kill it first. You would also have to tend to the home garden and livestock, if you had any.

And you're still not ready to begin cooking. You'd have to pump and haul water, carry coal, chop wood, and start and watch the fire. This last task was no small feat. Ovens had no handy thermometers or switches, so you had to know how to control the temperature by building the fire a certain way. That's why old recipes don't say, "Bake for 45 minutes at 350°F." Instead, their instructions are more like, "Bake in a quick oven till done." Helpful, right? Victorian cookbooks assume readers have a lot of prior knowledge, and they often don't list specific ingredient amounts either. That's why their directions can read like the Technical Challenge on *The Great British Baking Show*.

NOVEL TAKES ON CLASSIC RECIPES

The technical challenge of making a historical receipt (recipe) is fun, but can often be frustrating if you're not an experienced cook. In this book, we've tried as much as possible to keep to the flavors and textures of the actual food from the era, so that you can literally get a taste of what it was like to live 150 years ago. For the most part, we've been pleasantly surprised at how good Victorian food is—there's a perception that

---

3 Veit, *Food in the Civil War Era*, 24.

it's all flavorless boiled things, but these simple preparations really let the ingredients shine. Time after time we would read a recipe from an old cookbook and think that there was no possible way it would work, only to be shocked at how delicious it turned out to be.

We've made some modifications to ingredients where they're no longer readily available in the U.S. (mutton, black currants) or now known to be toxic (bitter almond) or prohibitively expensive (recipes containing truffles, or 100 oysters, were left out). We've also updated techniques since most people no longer have a smokehouse, a cooking fireplace with a roasting spit, or a special muslin bag for the purpose of boiling squash—not to mention an army of apprentice cooks to make French sauces, or a kitchen maid to whip egg whites by hand.

We've sprinkled a few original 19th-century receipts through this book so you can compare our modern versions, side by side. The main difference between our recipes and their historical counterparts is that we've tested ours, given specific measurements and clear instructions, and done our best to take out the guesswork so you can just go ahead and cook!

Note: Unless otherwise specified, we tested these recipes using:

- Salted butter (we believe in salted butter for almost everything!)
- Diamond Crystal kosher salt (the large crystals are less salty by volume than regular table salt, so use less if your salt is fine-grained)
- Unrefined cane sugar (rather than pure white, it's a golden color, with a hint of molasses—more flavorful and historically accurate, but regular white sugar is fine with no adjustments)

- All-purpose flour (flour production was a whole different thing back then, so we just went with what's easy to get)
- Large eggs (eggs were most likely smaller in the 1800s, but we've adjusted since small eggs are harder to find these days)

WHO IS MRS. CORNELIUS?

We consulted a wide variety of historical cookbooks in compiling these recipes, but one in particular stands out: *The Young Housekeeper's Friend*, first published in 1846. It is actually mentioned by name more than once in *Little Women*, so it became our first point of reference for the dishes in this book. And the author, Mary Hooker Cornelius, was from Andover, Massachusetts—not far from Concord, where Louisa May Alcott's family lived.

In the preface Mrs. Cornelius writes, "I have seen many a young lady, just entered upon the duties of married life, perplexed and prematurely care-worn, for want of experience, or a little good instruction, in regard to the simplest domestic processes; and often have felt, with the sincerest sympathy, an earnest wish to render her some effectual aid."

Her wish seems to have come true: The cookbook was quite popular in its day, and went through several editions—with good reason, as we discovered. Of all the cookbooks we used in our research, the receipts in this one were always the tastiest and most reliable!

As you go through our recipes, you'll see the occasional tip marked "Friendly Advice"—these are hints from us in the spirit of Mrs. Cornelius, to make your cooking easier, avoid disasters, or suggest alternative ways to serve a dish.

Which March Sister Are You?

Before we embark on our culinary journey, let's see if you're a Meg, Jo, Beth, or Amy. Take this personality quiz to find out! Here's what you do:

STEP 1: For each numbered statement, decide if you agree or disagree. Circle the letters in the column for your response.

STEP 2: Count the number of As that were circled and note it on the next page. Do the same for the Bs, Cs, and Ds.

STEP 3: Take a look on the next page to see which sister you are!

	AGREE		DISAGREE
1. I consider myself a creative person.	B D		A C
2. I like big social gatherings.	A B D		C
3. I've often dreamed of falling in love.	A		B C D
4. I love puttering around the house.	A C		B D
5. I seek adventure in my life.	B D		A C
6. I can't keep track of my stuff—I lose and break things all the time.	B		A C D
7. I admit I have a temper.	B D		A C
8. If I could choose, I'd live in a gorgeous mansion over a cute cottage.	A D		B C
9. I kind of enjoy shocking people.	B		A C D
10. I want to earn acclaim for my work.	B D		A C
11. Flirting is fun for me.	A D		B C
12. I'm always coming up with ideas.	B D		A C
13. I make friends easily.	A B D		C
14. My clothes are very important to me.	A D		B C
15. It's hard for me to say I'm sorry.	B D		A C

Number of As: _____ Number of Bs: _____ Number of Cs: _____ Number of Ds: _____

Each letter represents a March sister.
Which letter do you have the most of?

Mostly As

You are most like ... Meg!

Meg is sweet, patient, and domestic. These are characteristics she shares with Beth, but Meg is more social, flirtatious, and romantic. She appreciates nice things and little luxuries, especially clothes. Cook up a delicious dinner with Meg in Chapter 1 (page 12).

Mostly Bs

You are most like ... Jo!

Jo seeks adventure and dreams of accomplishing great things. A conventional life is not for Jo. She has a temper and can be heedless. Jo is a social creature and likes being around people (although she has a distaste for fancy company and occasions). Take a bite out of life with Jo's favorite foods in Chapter 2 (page 30).

Mostly Cs

You are most like ... Beth!

Beth is kind, careful, and considerate. She prefers to stay in a small circle of trusted loved ones than to go out among strangers. She likes being at home more than anywhere else. Enjoy a night in with Beth's cozy dishes and Victorian remedies in Chapter 3 (page 54).

Mostly Ds

You are most like ... Amy!

Like Jo, Amy is creative and adventurous, and she dreams of achieving greatness. Amy can be temperamental and has a weakness for pretty things. Popular and gifted with social grace, Amy enjoys parties, where she can be the belle of the ball. Indulge your inner Amy with treats in Chapter 4 (page 66).

If you take a look, the sisters have different traits they share with each of the others. Jo and Amy are often presented as opposites, so aren't you surprised, going through the questions, just how much they have in common? If Jo and Amy butt heads, it's not necessarily because they're too different!

Even if you get a perfect 15-point match on this quiz, none of us is a complete clone of any one March girl. The beauty of both the book's characters and ourselves is that we are multifaceted beings, and that means readers can find something to relate to in each of the four sisters.

CHAPTER 1

Meg

In spite of her small vanities, Margaret had a sweet and pious nature, which unconsciously influenced her sisters, especially Jo, who loved her very tenderly, and obeyed her because her advice was so gently given.

CHAPTER 2: "A MERRY CHRISTMAS"

Genteel, sentimental Meg longs for romance, beauty, and comfort. She loves parties, amateur theater, dressing up in pretty clothes, and adding little touches to make things nicer. As the oldest sister, she can still remember when their family had money, so she has the hardest time with their relative poverty. She can't afford new clothes, but she tries to remake her old ones to fit the latest the new fashions ... with mixed results. Eventually, she comes to realize that simplicity and good taste suit her best, and can be achieved even with her limited resources.

Despite her dreams of luxury, Meg defies even her own expectations by choosing love over money, and elects to be a poor man's wife. When she sets up her own household, she's willing to move into a small cottage and live a modest lifestyle in order to be with her beloved John Brooke, but she has high standards for herself as a housekeeper. She resolves that her home will always be perfectly clean and ready for unexpected company, with her as the perfect hostess in a pretty dress. (You can see where this is going—there's definitely going to be a day when her husband brings home a friend for dinner to find Meg sobbing into her apron, the kitchen a disaster, and the house in total disarray.)

Meg likes cooking, although she needs practice before she gets the hang of it. Young Meg proudly sends Laurie blanc-mange (page 84), her best dish, when he's sick, and tries to make an omelet for her mother (who very kindly does not tell her how badly it turned out). As a newly married woman, Meg is determined to master the culinary arts by working through every recipe in *The Young Housekeeper's Friend* book, and despite some embarrassing setbacks, she eventually does become a competent cook and homemaker, the kind of person friends and neighbors come to for advice and encouragement with their own domestic difficulties. She truly enjoys making her home a pleasant and beautiful place, with a happy family around her.

A modern Meg is the one who can throw a real dinner party, with hors d'oeuvres and cloth napkins. Her house is full of amazing vintage yard sale finds, and her kitchen is spotless when anyone comes over. If you're a close friend (or sister), you realize all these accomplishments don't always come easily—Meg is the queen of the Pinterest fail, but unlike Jo, she would never send photos of her latest hilarious disaster. Instead, Meg would toil in secret until she's able to produce a beautiful success.

In this chapter, we've included revisions of some of Meg's failed attempts, like the omelet that Marmee threw away and the currant jelly that wouldn't jell (this one will). You'll also find a selection of simple weekday recipes for the newlyweds, based on the classics that good Mrs. Cornelius wrote for the young housekeepers of the mid-1800s.

Omelet for Mother

There was plenty of food in the larder, and, while Beth and Amy set the table, Meg and Jo got breakfast, wondering, as they did so, why servants ever talked about hard work.

"I shall take some up to mother, though she said we were not to think of her, for she'd take care of herself," said Meg, who presided, and felt quite matronly behind the teapot.

So a tray was fitted out before anyone began, and taken up, with the cook's compliments. The boiled tea was very bitter, the omelet scorched, and the biscuits speckled with saleratus; but Mrs. March received her repast with thanks and laughed heartily over it after Jo was gone.

"Poor little souls, they will have a hard time, I'm afraid; but they won't suffer, and it will do them good," she said, producing the more palatable viands with which she had provided herself, and disposing of the bad breakfast, so that their feelings might not be hurt, —a motherly little deception, for which they were grateful.

CHAPTER II: "EXPERIMENTS"

Everyone has to start somewhere, and this is clearly Meg's first attempt at making breakfast. Never cook an omelet on high heat, or you'll end up with a scorched one like hers! It may sound strange to put nutmeg in a savory egg dish, but it adds a nice flavor, almost like a different sort of pepper.

Makes 1 serving

- 2 eggs
- 2 tablespoons milk
- 1 tablespoon minced onion
- ½ teaspoon freshly grated nutmeg
- pinch of salt
- ½ tablespoon butter, or as needed for frying

1. In a small bowl, beat the eggs and milk together with a fork until a bit frothy.

2. Add the onion, nutmeg, and salt and mix well.

3. Heat a small frying pan over medium heat and melt the butter in it. Make sure the butter coats the whole pan and goes up the sides a bit.

4. Pour in the egg mixture and put a lid on the pan. Let cook for 1 to 2 minutes, until the eggs are set around the edges but still a little loose in the middle.

5. Use a wide spatula to fold the omelet in half (it should be a little browned on the outside) and slide it onto a plate to serve.

Friendly Advice: Garnish with fresh herbs and the cook's compliments.

Meg

Domestic Experiences from the Dovecote

Like most other young matrons, Meg began her married life with the determination to be a model housekeeper. John should find home a paradise; he should always see a smiling face, should fare sumptuously every day, and never know the loss of a button. She brought so much love, energy, and cheerfulness to the work that she could not but succeed, in spite of some obstacles. Her paradise was not a tranquil one; for the little woman fussed, was over-anxious to please, and bustled about like a true Martha, cumbered with many cares. She was too tired, sometimes, even to smile; John grew dyspeptic after a course of dainty dishes, and ungratefully demanded plain fare.

CHAPTER 28: "DOMESTIC EXPERIENCES"

Meg and John start out their married life by "playing house," charmed by the idea of having their own household, with each trying their best to act out the role of husband or wife as they imagine they're supposed to do. Of course, real life isn't like that. Some

days the jelly doesn't jell, the salary isn't enough for a new overcoat, the kids won't stay in bed, the parents forget to talk to each other ... but these small setbacks ultimately bring them closer together, and they realize they need to participate in each other's lives and be equals rather than playing roles. As Marmee tells Meg, "Talk with him, let him read to you, exchange ideas, and help each other in that way. Don't shut yourself up in a bandbox because you are a woman, but understand what is going on, and educate yourself to take your part in the world's work, for it all affects you and yours."

The book doesn't always say exactly what Meg cooked for John, but we've put together a few ideas: the frugal but satisfying leftovers meal of beef hash and bread pudding, or the slightly daring mutton curry with rice, perhaps to add some spice to the relationship? Serve either meal with the simple and clever vegetable recipes that Mrs. Cornelius does so well.

Mathematical Mutton Curry

They were very happy, even after they discovered that they couldn't live on love alone. John did not find Meg's beauty diminished, though she beamed at him from behind the familiar coffee-pot; nor did Meg miss any of the romance from the daily parting, when her husband followed up his kiss with the tender inquiry, "Shall I send home veal or mutton for dinner, darling?" [...] While the cooking mania lasted she went through Mrs. Cornelius's Receipt Book as if it were a mathematical exercise, working out the problems with patience and care.

CHAPTER 28: "DOMESTIC EXPERIENCES"

We often think of Victorian-era food as plain and bland, but all kinds of ingredients and spices were being imported from India and Asia and were an important part of the cooking repertoire. As Meg worked her way through *The Young Housekeeper's Friend,* she would have come across this "Calcutta Curry." Mutton being hard to come by in the U.S. these days, we made the curry with lamb instead. This curry can be made ahead and will be even better the next day.

Makes 6 servings

For the curry:
- 2 pounds lamb shoulder chops
- 4 cups (1 quart) water
- 2 tablespoons butter
- 1 large onion, diced
- 2 tablespoons curry powder
  (or more to taste)
- ½ cup flour
- salt
- 1 lemon

For the rice:
- 2 cups long-grain rice
- 6 cups warm water
- 1 tablespoon kosher salt

PREPARE THE CURRY:

1. Cut the meat off the bones of the lamb shoulder chops. Put the bones and any other trimmings in a medium saucepan with the water over medium-low heat, and let them simmer while you prepare the other ingredients. Skim off any foam that appears.

2. Chop the meat into ½-inch cubes.

3. Melt the butter in a large pot over medium-high heat, then add the onions. Sauté until the onions are browned, about 5 minutes. (While the onions are cooking, start the rice.)

4. Add the curry powder and flour, and stir to coat the onions. Keep stirring for 1 to 2 minutes, until the flour is browning and starting to stick to the bottom of the pot. Be careful not to let it burn.

5. Add the cubed lamb and stir again until everything is evenly coated with the flour mixture and the lamb is starting to brown, about 3 minutes.

6. Pour the lamb broth through a strainer into the large pot with the other ingredients. Discard the bones and other trimmings. Stir well, scraping the bottom of the pot to combine all of the curry mixture.

7. Turn the heat to low and simmer until the sauce is thickened and the lamb is cooked through; 10 minutes should be enough to cook everything, but longer is better. Add salt to taste.

8. Serve over rice, with lemon wedges to squeeze over the top or lemon catsup (page 69).

PREPARE THE RICE:

1. Rinse the rice well in a strainer.

2. Put the water and salt in a large pot.

3. Add the rice and bring to a boil over high heat.

4. Reduce to a simmer and cook, uncovered, for 10 minutes, or until the rice is tender.

5. Drain through a sieve and fluff with a fork before serving.

Friendly Advice: Not a fan of lamb? You can substitute beef, chicken, or pork, and add potatoes and carrots if you'd like to add more substance to the meal.

Meg

Frugal Bread-Pudding and Hash

An evening with John over the account-books usually produced a temporary lull in the culinary enthusiasm, and a frugal fit would ensue, during which the poor man was put through a course of bread-pudding, hash, and warmed-over coffee, which tried his soul, although he bore it with praise-worthy fortitude.

CHAPTER 28: "DOMESTIC EXPERIENCES"

Bread-Pudding

This bread-pudding is less rich and sweet than modern versions, and is even better reheated the next day. The original recipe says to flavor the custard with peach leaves, but since those aren't always available, we used almond extract.

Makes 8 servings

- 4 cups (1 quart) milk
- 5 eggs
- 1 teaspoon nutmeg
- ½ teaspoon salt
- ⅓ cup sugar
- ½ teaspoon almond extract

- 2 tablespoons butter, softened, plus more for the pan
- 5 slices hearty white bread (Good Family Bread, page 108, is a good option)
- 1 cup finely chopped dried peaches, raisins, or other dried fruit

1. Heat the milk in a medium saucepan over medium heat.

2. Beat the eggs, nutmeg, salt, and sugar together in a small bowl.

3. Once the milk starts to bubble at the edges, turn the heat off and whisk ½ cup hot milk into the egg mixture, then another ½ cup, then pour all the egg mixture into the milk in the pan.

4. Heat on low, stirring constantly, until it's thick enough to coat the back of a spoon.

5. Immediately remove from the heat and pour into a large bowl, then stir in the almond extract.

6. Butter a 9 x 9-inch baking dish and preheat the oven to 350°F.

7. Butter each slice of bread then cut them into 1-inch pieces.

8. Add the bread pieces and the dried peaches or other dried fruit to the custard and mix well.

9. Pour everything into the baking dish and cover with foil.

10. Bake about 30 minutes, or until heated through and starting to bubble.

Friendly Advice: If you have access to a peach tree in the right season, instead of adding the almond extract, try steeping a handful of young leaves in the warm milk for a few minutes (not too long, or it will be bitter) before you make the custard.

Domestic Experiences.

Meg

Beef Hash

This is by no means an elegant dish—one would certainly not serve it if Mrs. Amy Laurence were coming to dine—but it's comforting and a good way to stretch leftover roast beef into a meal. Note: In the cookbooks of this era, "hash" is usually some sort of meat-and-gravy dish, rather than the meat-fried-with-potatoes diner food that's more common today.

Makes 2 servings

- 2 tablespoons butter
- 1 small onion, diced
- 2 tablespoons flour
- 2 cups beef stock
- 1 teaspoon cider vinegar
- 1 tablespoon minced parsley (optional)
- 1 sprig of thyme (optional)
- 1½ cups diced Roast Beef for Great Appetites (page 44), preferably cooked rare
- salt and pepper
- 2 slices toast (Good Family Bread, page 108, is a good option)

1. Melt the butter in a small frying pan over medium heat.

2. Add the onions, and cook till they have softened a bit and are becoming translucent, about 5 minutes.

3. Add the flour and stir till it becomes a paste. Let it cook for 1 minute.

4. Add the beef stock a little at a time, stirring to completely incorporate each addition before adding more. You should now have a nice gravy. If it's too thick, you can add water. If too thin, let it boil a little longer.

5. Add the vinegar, parsley, and thyme, if using, and beef. Turn down the heat and let everything warm through, but don't let it boil or the meat may become tough.

6. Taste, and add salt and pepper to your liking.

7. Serve in shallow bowls ladled over toast, or with the toast on the side for dipping if you prefer.

The Vegetables John Sent Home

"A man to dinner, and everything in a mess! John Brooke, how *could* you do such a thing?"

"I didn't know it this morning, and there was no time to send word, for I met him on the way out. I never thought of asking leave, when you have always told me to do as I liked. I never tried it before, and hang me if I ever do again!" added John, with an aggrieved air.

"I should hope not! Take him away at once; I can't see him, and there isn't any dinner."

"Well, I like that! Where's the beef and vegetables I sent home, and the pudding you promised?" cried John, rushing to the larder.

CHAPTER 28: "DOMESTIC EXPERIENCES"

Meg

Summer Squash

The original recipe says to "boil it whole, in a little bag kept for the purpose." The bag isn't really necessary, but squeezing out the water this way concentrates and improves the flavor of the squash. Look for squash with thin, tender skin.

Makes 4 servings

- 2 large yellow crookneck squash or 4 zucchini, about 1 pound
- 1 tablespoon butter
- salt

1. Put the squash whole into a large pot with enough water to cover.

2. Boil for 45 minutes (less if you have smaller squash), until very tender.

3. Remove the squash and put into a colander.

4. Use a smaller bowl to press out most of the liquid from the squash.

5. Transfer into a serving bowl, add butter and season to taste with salt, and mash well with a fork.

String Beans

You might think it sounds strange to add flour at the end, but it makes a nice sauce for the beans. Cutting them in little pieces also improves the dish; it seems to bring out the flavor of the beans.

Makes 4 servings

- 1 pound string beans
- ½ teaspoon kosher salt
- 2 tablespoons softened butter
- 2 tablespoons flour

1. Remove the ends of the beans, and cut them into ½-inch pieces.

2. Place in a medium saucepan with the salt and just enough water to barely cover.

3. Boil over high heat until bright green and tender, 5 to 10 minutes.

4. Turn the heat to low, add the butter and flour, and stir well until the sauce thickens, 1 to 2 minutes.

Currant Jelly for the Family Jar

Fired with a housewifely wish to see her store-room stocked with home-made preserves, she undertook to put up her own currant jelly. John was requested to order home a dozen or so of little pots, and an extra quantity of sugar, for their own currants were ripe, and were to be attended to at once. [...] Home came four dozen delightful little pots, half a barrel of sugar, and a small boy to pick the currants for her. With her pretty hair tucked into a little cap, arms bared to the elbow, and a checked apron which had a coquettish look in spite of the bib, the young housewife fell to work, feeling no doubts about her success; for hadn't she seen Hannah do it hundreds of times? The array of pots rather amazed her at first, but John was so fond of jelly, and the nice little jars would look so well on the top shelf, that Meg resolved to fill them all, and spent a long day picking, boiling, straining, and fussing over her jelly. She did her best; she asked advice of Mrs. Cornelius; she racked her brain to remember what Hannah did that she left undone; she reboiled, resugared, and restrained, but that dreadful stuff wouldn't "*jell.*"

CHAPTER 28: "DOMESTIC EXPERIENCES"

A jelly bag is nice to have for this—it's a muslin bag that hangs on a stand over a bowl, allowing the juice to drain out slowly without any pulp getting through. You can rig up a makeshift version by lining a colander with several layers of cheesecloth and setting it over a bowl.

1 pound of currants will make about 1 cup of jelly

- fresh or frozen red currants (not dried)
- white sugar to equal the weight of the juice from the currants

1. Rinse the currants and put them in a saucepan that would hold about twice their volume—stems, seeds, and all. Add a little water in the bottom of the pan, about ½ inch deep.

2. Set up the jelly bag over a bowl.

3. Cook the currants over medium heat, mashing with a potato masher or the back of a spoon, until the berries have released their juice. This will only take a few minutes.

4. Transfer the currants and juice to the jelly bag, and let it drain for several hours or overnight. Don't wring out the bag, or the jelly will be cloudy.

5. When you're ready to start cooking, put a small plate in the freezer.

6. Weigh the juice that drained out, and add the same weight of sugar.

7. Transfer the juice and sugar mixture to a saucepan and set it over medium heat.

8. Bring to a strong boil, with lots of bubbles all over the surface (but don't let it boil over).

9. Reduce heat to low and boil for 5 to 10 minutes, stirring often, until you can see it starting to thicken a bit when you let it run off the spoon, or until it reaches 220°F on a candy thermometer (an instant-read or laser thermometer doesn't work well for this).

10. Test the jelly by dropping a small spoonful on the cold plate and putting it back in the freezer for 1 minute. Take it out again and push your finger through the jelly on the plate. If it wrinkles as you push it, it's done. If not, keep boiling and try again in a few minutes.

11. Once done, transfer the jelly to a jar through a fine-mesh strainer and process it for canning if you like, or just store it in the refrigerator (it will last for up to three months).

Friendly Advice: Making jelly is easy—it's just equal weights of juice and sugar, so you almost don't need a recipe. Currants have a lot of pectin, so they should jell up nicely, despite poor Meg's difficulties. Mrs. Cornelius warns that you shouldn't stop boiling the jelly once you've started—maybe that was Meg's problem?

Meg

Demi's Little Cakes

Meg slipped away, and ran down to greet her husband with a smiling face, and the little blue bow in her hair which was his especial admiration. He saw it at once and said with pleased surprise,—"Why, little mother, how gay we are tonight. Do you expect company?"

"Only you, dear."

"Is it a birthday, anniversary, or anything?"

"No; I'm tired of being dowdy, so I dressed up as a change. You always make yourself nice for table, no matter how tired you are; so why shouldn't I when I have the time?"

"I do it out of respect for you, my dear," said old-fashioned John.

"Ditto, ditto, Mr. Brooke," laughed Meg, looking young and pretty again, as she nodded to him over the teapot.

"Well, it's altogether delightful, and like old times. This tastes right. I drink your health, dear." And John sipped his tea with an air of reposeful rapture, which was of very short duration, however; for, as he put down his cup, the door-handle rattled mysteriously, and a little voice was heard, saying impatiently,—

"Opy doy; me's tummin!"

"It's that naughty boy. I told him to go to sleep alone, and here he is, downstairs, getting his death a-cold pattering over that canvas," said Meg, answering the call.

"Mornin' now," announced Demi in joyful tone, as he entered, with his long night-gown gracefully festooned over his arm, and every curl bobbing gayly as he pranced about the table, eyeing the "cakies" with loving glances.

"No, it isn't morning yet. You must go to bed, and not trouble poor mamma; then you can have the little cake with sugar on it."

CHAPTER 38: "ON THE SHELF"

These turn out fluffy and lemony; they would serve equally well as a nice dessert for a romantic evening or a bribe for a toddler who won't stay in bed.

Makes 12 cupcakes

- ½ cup butter
- ¼ teaspoon kosher salt
- 1 cup sugar, plus more for sprinkling
- 2 whole eggs plus 1 egg yolk
- zest and juice of ½ lemon
- 1¾ cups flour
- ½ cup buttermilk
- ½ teaspoon baking soda

1. Have all the ingredients at room temperature.

2. Preheat the oven to 350°F and line a muffin tin with paper liners.

3. In the bowl of a stand mixer fitted with the paddle attachment, cream the butter, salt and sugar together until well combined.

4. Add the eggs and lemon zest. Whip on high speed for 3 to 5 minutes, until it's light-colored and fluffy.

5. Add half the flour, mix, then add the buttermilk, mix, then add the rest of the flour with the baking soda.

6. Add the lemon juice and stir to combine.

7. Portion the batter into the muffin cups. Fill only three-quarters full.

8. Lightly grease the top of the muffin tin in case they spill over.

9. Bake about 18 minutes, until the tops are set and edges are just browning.

10. Immediately after removing them from the oven, sprinkle the tops with sugar.

Meg

CHAPTER 2

Jo

But you see, Jo wasn't a heroine; she was only a struggling human girl like hundreds of others, and she just acted out her nature, being sad, cross, listless, or energetic, as the mood suggested.

CHAPTER 42: "ALL ALONE"

Jo is probably your favorite, and why wouldn't she be? She's talented, literary, kind-hearted, loyal, and generous, but just like a real person she's also bad-tempered, impatient, headstrong, and in a constant state of chaos. Who doesn't relate to that?

It's no surprise that generations of little women have identified with Jo's struggle to fit herself into the conventional image of femininity—the ideal is always changing, and always unattainable. She is absolutely incapable of being anything other than authentic at all times, which is both endearing and frustrating for those who love her. She's constantly getting in her own way, saying the wrong thing at the worst possible time, and scandalizing polite society with her lack of manners, boyish appearance, and general inability to act like a proper young lady.

On the other hand, Jo does have domestic skills—she sews most of her sisters' dresses, and is an excellent wrangler of children. With her father away in the war, she calls herself the "man of the family" and does her best to look after her mother and sisters. When Beth is ill, Jo stays by her side night and day, caring for her tenderly until the end. Jo may be topsy-turvy, but underneath everything, she's a total softie; as Meg says, "like a chestnut burr, prickly outside, but silky-soft within, and a sweet kernel, if one can only get at it."

Eating is simply a practicality for Jo; she only learns to cook because it's necessary for basic survival. She'll occasionally take on a cooking project as a personal challenge, but Jo doesn't have the patience and foresight required to pull off anything complicated. We can see modern-day Jo living a happy, gender-nonconforming life with her kitchen cupboards full of books and half-finished projects, and her freezer stuffed with homemade meals from Beth and Marmee because she is one of those people who always forgets to eat. Amy drags her out to try the latest food trends, but Jo's too busy thinking about her students or her writing to notice what she's eating, and anyway, she'd prefer a nice crisp apple to any elaborate patisserie.

The recipes in Jo's chapter are straightforward and tasty, like the gingerbread that's one of the only things she knows how to cook. There's a menu for a festive dinner party: Jo's attempt is such a disaster that it becomes a family joke, but with modernized recipes and the benefit of our experience, you can pull it off easily. And the warm, nourishing boarding-house dinner that ends in an any-season peach pie showcases simple flavors in a way that our modern palates don't often experience. Not to mention, it makes great brain fuel for writing about gruesome murders and tragic romances.

Gingerbread That's Fit to Eat

"Don't try too many messes, Jo, for you can't make anything but gingerbread and molasses candy fit to eat."

CHAPTER II: "EXPERIMENTS"

Jo's not the best of cooks, and when she starts getting carried away by grand plans for a dinner, Meg reminds her that her repertoire is very limited. Gingerbread is the most frequently mentioned food in *Little Women* and comes in many forms. This one is a dark, intense ginger cake with a strong molasses flavor—spicy and not too sweet.

Makes 1 (9 x 5-inch) loaf

- 2 tablespoons water
- 1 teaspoon baking soda
- ½ cup butter, plus more for greasing
- ½ teaspoon salt
- 1 cup molasses
- 3 scant cups flour
- 1 tablespoon ground ginger
- 1 teaspoon ground cinnamon
- ½ teaspoon ground cloves
- ½ cup packed dark brown sugar
- 2 eggs
- 1 cup buttermilk

1. Preheat the oven to 350°F. Grease a 9 x 5-inch loaf pan.

2. In a small pot, boil the water and mix in the baking soda.

3. Add the butter and salt, then stir until the butter melts.

4. Stir in molasses and whisk together. Let cool while you get the dry ingredients together.

5. In a large bowl, whisk the flour, ginger, cinnamon, and cloves together, then whisk in the sugar.

6. In a medium bowl, whisk the eggs and buttermilk together, then add the molasses mixture and stir to combine.

7. Pour the wet ingredients into the dry ingredients and stir well.

8. Pour the batter into the prepared pan and bake for about 1 hour, until the bread just begins to pull away from the edge of the pan. A toothpick inserted in the center should come out clean.

9. Remove from oven and cool on a rack for at least 15 minutes before serving. This bread tastes best the next day.

Old-Fashioned Measurements

Nineteenth-century cookbooks often list old-fashioned measurements, which are quaint and fun to read, but not terribly helpful if you're trying to actually cook from them. We've made all the necessary modifications for the recipes in this book, but if you're ever looking to try your hand at a vintage recipe, here's a list of conversions for some of the most common terms:

- 60 drops = 1 teaspoon of liquid
- Butter the size of a nut or walnut = 2 tablespoons
- Butter the size of an egg = ½ cup
- Coffee cup = 1 cup
- Dash = ⅛ teaspoon
- Dessert spoon = 2 teaspoons
- Gill = ½ cup
- Lump of butter = 2 tablespoons
- Pinch = 1/16 teaspoon
- Salt spoon = ¼ teaspoon
- Teacup = ¾ cup
- Tin cup = 1 cup
- Tumblerful = 2 cups
- Wineglass = ¼ cup

Jo's Standing Joke of a Dinner

Despair seized them, when, a few minutes later, Miss Crocker appeared, and said she'd come to dinner. Now, this lady was a thin, yellow spinster, with a sharp nose, and inquisitive eyes, who saw everything, and gossiped about all she saw. They disliked her, but had been taught to be kind to her, simply because she was old and poor, and had few friends. So Meg gave her the easy-chair, and tried to entertain her, while she asked questions, criticised everything, and told stories of the people whom she knew.

Language cannot describe the anxieties, experiences, and exertions which Jo underwent that morning; and the dinner she served up became a standing joke. Fearing to ask any more advice, she did her best alone, and discovered that something more than energy and good-will is necessary to make a cook. [...]

Poor Jo would gladly have gone under the table, as one thing after another was tasted and left; while Amy giggled, Meg looked distressed, Miss Crocker pursed her lips, and Laurie talked and laughed with all his might, to give a cheerful tone to the festive scene. [...]

[Jo] turned scarlet, and was on the verge of crying, when she met Laurie's eyes, which *would* look merry in spite of his heroic efforts; the comical side of the affair suddenly struck her, and she laughed till the tears ran down her cheeks. So did every one else, even "Croaker," as the girls called the old lady; and the unfortunate dinner ended gayly, with bread and butter, olives and fun.

CHAPTER II: "EXPERIMENTS"

We've all been there: At one point or another, we've gotten overconfident, invited a bunch of guests over, promised an impressive feast that's beyond our skill ... and ended up with an embarrassing, inedible waste of ingredients and time, along with a kitchen covered in dirty dishes and cooking residue. We feel your pain, Jo!

We do admire Jo's taste in menu planning, even though she didn't have the expertise or experience to match her vision. This is a great, well-rounded meal for friends—a comforting, nourishing treat without being overly fussy. Jo's standing joke of a dinner features corned beef, boiled potatoes, asparagus, lobster salad, bread (page 108) and butter, blanc-mange (page 84), and strawberries and cream.

Corned Beef

"Well, they can eat beef, and bread and butter, if they are hungry; only it's mortifying to have to spend your whole morning for nothing," thought Jo, as she rang the bell half an hour later than usual, and stood, hot, tired, and dispirited, surveying the feast spread for Laurie, accustomed to all sorts of elegance, and Miss Crocker, whose curious eyes would mark all failures, and whose tattling tongue would report them far and wide.

CHAPTER 11: "EXPERIMENTS"

The "corn" in corned beef actually refers to the kernels of salt that were used to preserve it—there's no corn in it at all! Nowadays most corned beef is brined with a variety of spices, but recipes from the 19th century just used salt, saltpeter (similar to modern curing salt), water, and sometimes molasses. We were surprised to find that this version doesn't taste much different from the modern spiced one—you do taste the molasses, but it's not sweet and it still has the distinctive corned beef flavor and color.

Before refrigeration, you would be careful to only make this when the weather was cool, but now we have a handy eternal winter in the refrigerator and can happily make corned beef in July if we feel like it.

Makes 6 to 8 servings

- 8 cups (2 quarts) water
- 1½ cups salt
- 2 tablespoons pink curing salt
- ½ cup molasses
- 1 beef brisket, about 5 pounds

- 4 cups ice
- 2 bay leaves (optional)
- 1 teaspoon black peppercorns (optional)
- carrots, potatoes, cabbage, for serving (optional)

AT LEAST 10 DAYS BEFORE YOU WANT TO EAT:

(If you have an already-corned beef, skip ahead to the cooking stage.)

1. Combine the water, salt, pink curing salt, and molasses in a large stock pot that will hold the brisket and will fit in your refrigerator. Heat on high until the salt and molasses are dissolved, then remove from heat and allow to cool.

2. Rinse the brisket and trim off some of the fat cap if you like, but leave a ½-inch layer at least. Trim off any silver skin or gristle on the outside.

3. Add the ice to the brine in the pot, and stir until the mixture is completely cold.

4. Put the brisket in the pot, making sure it's completely submerged. If it wants to float, place a ceramic bowl or other heavy, nonreactive object on top to keep it under the brine.

5. Put the whole contraption in the refrigerator and leave it for 10 to 14 days (go for the longer end if your brisket is especially thick). Check on it every day or so and flip the meat over so it brines evenly.

WHEN YOU ARE READY TO COOK THE BEEF:

1. Pour off the brine and rinse the brisket well. Wash the pot.

2. Return the brisket to the clean pot and fill it with enough water to cover the meat by an inch or so. Add the bay leaves and peppercorns, if using.

3. Simmer over low heat so the water is barely bubbling for about 5 hours, until fork-tender, or 145°F in the center of the brisket. Check occasionally and add more water as needed.

4. In the last 30 minutes of cooking, you can add vegetables if you like, starting with carrots, then potatoes, then cabbage.

Lobster Salad

The salad-dressing so aggravated her, that she let everything else go till she had convinced herself that she could not make it fit to eat. The lobster was a scarlet mystery to her, but she hammered and poked, till it was unshelled, and its meagre proportions concealed in a grove of lettuce-leaves.

CHAPTER II: "EXPERIMENTS"

This makes an elegant presentation of lettuce topped with lobster and drizzled with a creamy, tangy sauce. Despite Jo's aggravation, the dressing is particularly good, and also goes well on the boiled potatoes (or eaten with a spoon).

One small lobster will serve about two people. Adjust the water and salt as needed depending on how many you're serving. Note: Lobsters must be alive when you cook them. Don't put ice on them or put them in fresh water—this will kill them.

Makes 2 servings

For the dressing:
- 4 eggs
- 3 tablespoons olive oil
- ⅓ cup white vinegar
- 1 teaspoon freshly ground pepper
- 1 tablespoon whole-grain mustard
- ½ teaspoon kosher salt
- fresh lemon juice to taste (optional)

For the salad:
- 3 quarts (12 cups) water
- 3 tablespoons kosher salt
- 1 small lobster (1½ to 2 pounds) per two people, or however many you can afford
- cool water (3 quarts per 1½ to 2 pounds of lobster)
- salt (1 tablespoon for every quart of water)
- 6 to 8 leaves butter lettuce
- freshly ground pepper for every pound of lobster

PREPARE THE DRESSING:

1. Cover the eggs with cold water in a large saucepan over high heat. Turn the heat off as soon as the water comes to a full boil. Let the eggs sit in the hot water to cook fully, 15 minutes to get to hard-boiled.

2. Take out the egg yolks, allow them to cool, and mash them in a small bowl.

Discard the whites or use them to decorate the salad.

3. Add olive oil, vinegar, mustard, freshly ground pepper, and salt in small increments to taste. Fresh lemon juice isn't in the original recipe, but it's very nice with the lobster. Add it as desired.

PREPARE THE SALAD:

1. Bring the water and salt (1 tablespoon per quart) to a rolling boil in a pot large enough that the lobster will be fully submerged and have a bit of extra room. If you would like to kill the lobster humanely, place the lobster in the freezer for 10 minutes, right before cooking.

2. Drop the lobster in the water headfirst, using tongs. Don't cover the pot.

3. Stir the lobster halfway through boiling. Boiled lobsters will be bright red when done. Boiling times depend on the weight of the total amount of lobster you have (not individual weight):

- 1 pound: 5 to 7 minutes
- 1¼ pounds: 7 to 8 minutes
- 1½ pounds: 8 to 10 minutes
- 2 pounds: 10 to 12 minutes
- 3 pounds: 12 to 14 minutes

4. Place the boiled lobsters in cool water until they are cool enough to crack and remove the meat.

5. Dice the lobster meat and arrange it on the lettuce leaves.

6. Drizzle the dressing over the lobster, and serve with freshly ground pepper.

Plenty of Potatoes

The potatoes had to be hurried, not to keep the asparagus waiting, and were not done at last.

CHAPTER II: "EXPERIMENTS"

A nice simple boiled potato with plenty of butter is a satisfying side, as long as you cook them all the way through.

Makes 4 servings

- 4 large russet potatoes or 8 small waxy potatoes
- 2 tablespoons salt
- water
- butter, for the table

1. Peel the potatoes if you prefer, and cut them in halves or quarters depending on size.

2. Put the potatoes in a large pot with the salt and fill the pot three-quarters full with water.

3. Heat on high until it comes to a boil, then reduce to medium and boil until the potatoes are tender, 15 to 25 minutes. Check for doneness by pulling one out and cutting it in half to see if the middle is cooked through.

4. Drain the water off, and shake the potatoes in the pot over medium-high heat to let them dry, then serve with butter as you like.

Boiled Asparagus

She boiled the asparagus for an hour, and was grieved to find the heads cooked off and the stalks harder than ever.

CHAPTER 11: "EXPERIMENTS"

When we first read this recipe in *The Young Housekeeper's Friend*, we could not imagine how it would be anything more than a giant pile of mush. But once we tasted it, we were amazed—each ingredient contributes something and it all adds up to delicious. The original version has you tie the asparagus in little bundles with string, but it's not really necessary. Everything else is just as Mrs. Cornelius said.

Makes 4 servings

- 1 pound asparagus, tough ends snapped off
- 1 tablespoon kosher salt
- 4 slices sturdy white bread
- 2 tablespoons softened butter

1. Put the asparagus in a large pot over high heat, with the salt and enough water to cover by about an inch. Boil until quite soft, 15 to 25 minutes, depending how thick the asparagus are.

2. While the asparagus is cooking, toast the bread.

3. Have four small plates and the softened butter handy.

4. When the asparagus is nearly done (overcooked by modern standards), quickly dip each slice of bread into the asparagus water, lay it on the plate, and spread it with butter.

5. Lay a portion of asparagus on each slice of bread, dot with a tiny bit more butter, and serve.

6. Eat with knife and fork.

Friendly Advice: Make sure your asparagus is fresh, and get the best bread and butter you can—it makes all the difference. Good Family Bread (page 108) works well, or opt for a crusty artisan loaf.

Jo

Mrs. Kirke's Five O'Clock Dinner

"Mrs. Kirke asked me if I wouldn't go down to the five o'clock dinner; and, feeling a little bit homesick, I thought I would, just to see what sort of people are under the same roof with me …. [Mrs. Kirke] gave me a seat by her, and after my face cooled off, I plucked up courage, and looked about me. [...]

"Cast away at the very bottom of the table was the Professor, shouting answers to the questions of a very inquisitive, deaf old gentleman on one side, and talking philosophy with a Frenchman on the other. If Amy had been here, she'd have turned her back on him forever, because, sad to relate, he had a great appetite, and shovelled in his dinner in a manner which would have horrified 'her ladyship'. I didn't mind, for I like 'to see folks eat with a relish', as Hannah says, and the poor man must have needed a deal of food after teaching idiots all day."

CHAPTER 33: "JO'S JOURNAL"

Jo sets out for a winter in New York, anxious to see and learn new things (and to take a break from Laurie, who's obviously into her in a way she can't reciprocate). She's signed up for a job as a governess and seamstress at a boarding house, which is like a dorm for strangers in the city. Jo's lucky in her choice of employer, Mrs. Kirke, who's a friend of Marmee's and a kindly woman who makes her feel right at home. Boarding house landladies aren't often known for their generosity or delicious food, but Mrs. Kirke seems to be an exception.

Jo doesn't describe what exactly they eat, but we can take a good guess at what they might have had for a 5 o'clock dinner in November. Mrs. Kirke would've probably provided some boarding house staples but added variety with a few more seasonal vegetables. Beef was ubiquitous on the common dining table, usually as a simple roast, stew, or steak, since poultry was expensive and a pain to prep. There was often pie, but fresh fruit was hard to come by, especially in late fall,[4] so give this dried peach pie a try. Boarding houses were known for their bad table manners,[5] so the best way to enjoy this dinner is to forget about being polite, shovel down your food, and eat with a relish!

---

4   Wendy Gamber, *The Boardinghouse in Nineteenth-Century America* (Baltimore: Johns Hopkins University Press, 2007), 79.
5   Gamber, *The Boardinghouse*, 92.

Roast Beef for Great Appetites

You can of course use any recipe you like for roast beef, but this method is closer to what they would have used back then, minus a roasting spit. Be sure to look for a rump roast with a good amount of fat on top.

Makes 6 to 8 servings

- 1 boneless rump roast, 3 to 4 pounds
- 2 tablespoons kosher salt
- ¼ cup lard or bacon fat, melted
- ¼ cup flour

1. Tie the roast with string to make it an even shape and prevent some parts from cooking faster than others. Butchers will sometimes do this for you if you ask!

2. Pat the beef dry and rub with the salt.

3. Leave uncovered in the fridge for a few hours or overnight if possible.

4. Place an oven rack in the second position from the bottom. It is also helpful to take the top rack of the oven out to make room. Preheat the oven to 225°F.

5. Set a wire rack in a rimmed baking sheet.

6. Melt the lard or bacon fat in a small saucepan and keep it handy, along with a basting brush.

7. Brush the rack with lard to keep the beef from sticking.

8. Place the beef, fat cap up, on the rack. Baste it with lard, then put it in the oven.

9. Every 20 minutes, baste the meat again with the lard.

10. Roast until the internal temperature at the thickest part reaches 120°F to 125°F, 60 to 90 minutes depending on the thickness of your roast. (This should give you a medium-rare roast, 130°F to 135°F, after the browning process. If you like yours more done, roast longer.)

11. Remove the roast from the oven and sprinkle it generously all over with flour, then baste again.

12. Switch the oven to broil, and broil the roast all over, turning as needed, until the flour froths up and browns slightly.

13. At this point, if you're feeling brave, and if there are some nice drippings in the pan, you can try an exciting historical gravy method: Boil a cup or two of water and pour it slowly over the roast, washing the browned flour off into the pan below. Then remove the roast and rack and put the pan on the stove, and cook the liquid with the flour, stirring constantly, until thickened. Add salt and pepper as needed. If you're not used to making gravy, however, we would skip this step.

14. Transfer the roast to a cutting board and let it rest for a few minutes before slicing. Try to slice against the grain of the meat.

Friendly Advice: Do you have leftovers? Use them to make a beef hash (page 22) the next day!

Mashed Turnips

These days, many people have never eaten a turnip, and most likely think of them as the sort of thing characters in fairytales trade for magic beans. But they are in fact delicious either raw or cooked, with an unusual sweet and sharp flavor similar to a radish. Choose the smaller ones; they're more tender. Mashed turnips make an interesting alternative to mashed potatoes if you're looking for something less starchy.

Makes 4 servings

- 2 pounds turnips, peeled and quartered
- salt
- 3 tablespoons butter

1. Put the turnips, enough cold water to cover them, and a few tablespoons of salt in a large pot.

2. Turn the stove on high. When the water begins boiling, reduce to medium-high and cook, covered, for 30 minutes or until the turnips are very tender.

3. Drain and press the water out. Mash the turnips very well with a potato masher. There may be some stringy bits stuck in the masher—don't put them back in with the turnips!

4. Add the butter and salt to taste.

Friendly Advice: If there's excess water after draining, put the mash back into the pot over medium-high heat for 2 to 3 minutes, stirring constantly to keep it from burning, until the extra liquid has cooked off.

Stewed Onions to Eat with a Relish

This dish seems to have had a bad reputation—places like boarding houses and tenements were often described as smelling unpleasantly of stewed onions, and nowadays it's difficult to find much mention of it in cookbooks at all. This version, on the other hand, is delicious and even delicate; the onions become sweet and tender, a perfect side for a Sunday roast.

Makes 4 servings

- 14 ounces small white boiling onions (pearl or cippolini onions will also work)
- ⅓ cup water, plus more for boiling the onions
- ⅓ cup milk
- 1 tablespoon butter
- salt and pepper

1. Cut off the tops and bottoms of the onions, and pull off as much skin as comes off easily.

2. In a medium pot, start the onions in enough cold salted water to cover, and boil for 20 minutes, until translucent.

3. Drain completely, and remove any remaining skins.

4. Return the onions to the pot. Add ⅓ cup water, milk, and another pinch of salt. Simmer, uncovered, over low heat for 20 minutes, until the liquid is thickened a bit but not curdled.

5. Add the butter, and season to taste with salt and pepper.

Dried Peach Pie

Why restrict yourself to peach pie only in the summer? Dried peaches are made from fruit at the peak of ripeness, and the drying process seems to concentrate the pectin, resulting in a pie that holds together nicely and has an intense peach flavor.

Makes 6 servings

- 1 pound dried peaches, diced
- zest of 1 lemon
- pinch of salt
- 2 tablespoons sugar, or to taste, plus more for sprinkling
- lemon juice, as needed
- 1 Double Pie Crust (see page 50) or store-bought pie crust
- 1 egg, beaten

PREPARE THE FILLING:

1. Combine the peaches with about double their volume of water in a large saucepan and bring to a boil.

2. As soon as it comes to a boil, remove from heat and add the lemon zest and salt.

3. Let the peaches sit for 30 minutes or so, stirring occasionally, until they have absorbed most of the water.

4. Taste and add sugar and/or lemon juice as needed—depending on the type of peaches you have, they may be more sweet or more sour.

5. Let the peach mixture cool completely while you prepare the pie crust. (Or you can make the filling ahead and refrigerate it.) You may need to add more water—there should be some juice, but it should be thick, not watery.

ASSEMBLE AND BAKE THE PIE:

1. Preheat the oven to 400°F and set a rack in the lowest position.

2. Divide the pie dough in half and roll each half into a disk about ¼-inch thick.

3. Lay the bottom crust in a 9-inch pie pan and spoon in the filling.

4. Lay the top crust over the filling and crimp the edges tightly. If you're feeling ambitious, you can make a lattice crust, but a plain one works just fine here.

5. Brush the top crust with the beaten egg, then sprinkle generously with sugar.

6. If you're not making a lattice, cut vents in the crust with a small knife.

7. Bake on the lowest rack in the oven until the crust is golden brown, about 30 minutes. If the edges are cooking too quickly, cover them with foil.

8. Allow to cool before serving.

Friendly Advice: Though it's not part of the original recipe, adding a few dried apricots in the mix, about ½ cup, gives an extra layer of complexity, and whipped cream flavored with almond extract is an excellent accompaniment.

Double Pie Crust

Makes 2 (9-inch) pie crusts

- 2½ cups plus 2 tablespoons flour, divided
- 1 cup (2 sticks) plus 1 tablespoon butter, chilled and diced, divided
- ¼ cup ice water

1. In a large bowl, combine 2½ cups of the flour and the salt.

2. Cut the 1 cup diced butter into the flour (either with two knives or with your fingertips) until it resembles coarse crumbs.

3. Stir in the ice water, 1 tablespoon at a time, until the mixture forms a ball.

4. Roll out the dough and spread 1 tablespoon of butter, shaved into thin strips using a vegetable peeler, over the dough. Sprinkle the remaining 2 tablespoons of flour over the butter shavings.

5. Roll the dough up into a scroll, and then fold in half and press together. Wrap dough in plastic and refrigerate for 1 hour before rolling out.

Get the Receipt

Here is some of Mrs. Cornelius's excellent advice on making pastry (you'll notice that soggy bottoms were a concern back then just like today):

- There is hardly another article of food in which so much is sacrificed to appearance as in pastry. Everybody likes a light crust, a little brown, and not excessively rich, better than one that is half butter or lard, and baked white.

- The best-looking pastry is made with lard, but it is not so healthy or good, as that which is made with half or two thirds butter.

- It is difficult to make flaky crust in warm weather. But cooling the butter and water with ice, and having the pastry-table in the cellar, will insure tolerable success.

- A clammy lower-crust is neither good or digestible. Therefore never fill pies made of moist materials until just before putting them into the oven.

Seed-Cakes for the "Nargerie"

When I got back to the nursery there was such an uproar in the parlor that I looked in; and there was Mr. Bhaer down on his hands and knees, with Tina on his back, Kitty leading him with a jump-rope, and Minnie feeding two small boys with seed-cakes, as they roared and ramped in cages built of chairs.

"We are playing *nargerie*," explained Kitty.

"Dis is mine effalunt!" added Tina, holding on by the Professor's hair.

"Mamma always allows us to do what we like Saturday afternoon, when Franz and Emil come, doesn't she, Mr. Bhaer?" said Minnie.

"The 'effalunt' sat up, looking as much in earnest as any of them, and said soberly to me,—"I gif you my wort it is so, if we make too large a noise you shall say "Hush!" to us, and we go more softly."

CHAPTER 33: "JO'S JOURNAL"

There are a lot of different types of seed-cakes, from a whole loaf cake to something more like a cookie. This version makes cute little cakes that small imaginary lions would be happy to devour.

Makes about 12

- 1 tablespoon caraway seeds
- boiling water
- 8 ounces butter plus more for greasing the pans
- 8 ounces (1 cup) sugar
- 4 eggs
- 2 tablespoons brandy (optional)
- 8 ounces (2¼ cups) flour
- ½ teaspoon kosher salt
- ½ teaspoon ground mace

1. Have all the ingredients at room temperature.

2. Preheat the oven to 350°F.

3. Put the caraway seeds in a small, heatproof dish and pour a few tablespoons of boiling water on them; let them sit while you mix the rest of the ingredients.

5. In the bowl of a stand mixer fitted with the paddle attachment, cream the butter and sugar together until light and fluffy.

6. Add the eggs and brandy, if using, and whip on high speed for 3 minutes until smooth and light.

7. In a medium bowl, mix the flour, salt, and mace together, then add to the egg mixture in four parts, mixing on medium speed until just combined.

8. Stir in the caraway seeds and any remaining liquid.

9. Portion the batter into greased muffin tins or other small cake pans, filling them three-quarters full.

10. Bake for 15 to 20 minutes, until a skewer inserted into the middle comes out clean.

Jo

CHAPTER 3

Beth

She was a housewifely little creature, and helped Hannah keep home neat and comfortable for the workers, never thinking of any reward but to be loved. Long, quiet days she spent, not lonely nor idle, for her little world was peopled with imaginary friends, and she was by nature a busy bee.

Chapter 4: "Burdens"

Beth is like a warm, rosy lamp—a cozy presence that makes a house a home. When she's gone, the room feels suddenly cold and dark. We readers don't get to know Beth so much directly, but rather by seeing how she affects the people around her, particularly Jo. Beth is the only sister who doesn't get multiple chapters in the book devoted to her personal experience, and she's so focused on the wants and needs of others that she reveals little about herself. But here are some endearing contradictions we observe about Beth: She considers herself stupid, but she has great talent and passion for music. She thinks she's unimportant, but her family relies on her for comfort and support. She's intensely shy, but she'll step up and reach out if someone needs her help. And she trusts only a small circle of loved ones, but there are a surprising number of people around town who regard her as the kindest of friends.

A domestic little being, Beth plays an active role in the March family food scene. While she's healthy, she goes marketing and helps Hannah around the kitchen daily, and we bet she makes little snacks for her sisters (especially for Jo when she's holed up in the attic writing). Beth's a girl of simple tastes; her favorite treat is fresh fruit. The dishes she likes best are humdrum yet heartening—perfect for eating by a crackling fire, wrapped up in quilts and surrounded by her sisters and parents: toast, for example, and

the baked squash from the May 20 edition of *The Pickwick Portfolio*. When Beth is ill, she's offered more elaborate dishes, not because she wants fancy food, but because her family and friends need to channel all the love and fear and helplessness they're feeling into tangible gifts they can cook for her. This chapter includes recipes for Victorian remedies for the sick—some refreshing, others hearty and nourishing, and still others that are odd but worth a try.

The Beths of today would rather stay in for popcorn and board games than go out. At a potluck, they are the ones who quietly remember to bring the plates and napkins everyone else forgot, instead of baking a showstopper cake to impress. Our Beths are cheerful bearers of emotional labor, who will make you macaroni and cheese and brownies if you're having a bad day, and show up with a thermos of chicken soup when you're under the weather. Comfort food is their specialty, although they get the most enjoyment out of giving it to others, rather than eating it themselves.

Toast for Tea

"I'll tell you what we'll do," said Beth; "let's each get her something for Christmas, and not get anything for ourselves."

"That's like you, dear! What will we get?" exclaimed Jo.

Every one thought soberly for a minute; then Meg announced, as if the idea was suggested by the sight of her own pretty hands, "I shall give her a nice pair of gloves."

"Army shoes, best to be had," cried Jo.

"Some handkerchiefs, all hemmed," said Beth.

"I'll get a little bottle of cologne; she likes it, and it won't cost much, so I'll have some left to buy my pencils," added Amy.

"How will we give the things?" asked Meg.

"Put them on the table, and bring her in and see her open the bundles. Don't you remember how we used to do on our birthdays?" answered Jo.

"I used to be *so* frightened when it was my turn to sit in the chair with the crown on, and see you all come marching round to give the presents, with a kiss. I liked the things and the kisses, but it was dreadful to have you sit looking at me while I opened the bundles," said Beth, who was toasting her face and the bread for tea at the same time.

CHAPTER I: "PLAYING PILGRIMS"

As the March household's little Vesta, Beth is in the habit of making everyone their late meal on the hearth. This toast that Beth might have prepared is a cheesy comfort food that's perfect for cold nights. Good Family Bread (page 108), is perfect for this, or another hearty bread.

Back before oven broilers, you would use something called a salamander to brown the top of a dish—it was sort of like a fireplace poker, but with a wide flat disk of iron at the bottom. You would heat the disk up in the fire till it was red hot, then hold it over whatever you wanted to cook. Clever!

Makes 4 servings

- 4 slices bread
- ¼ cup (½ stick) softened butter
- 1 teaspoon whole grain mustard
- 1½ cups shredded sharp cheddar cheese

1. Preheat the oven to 350°F. Toast your bread on the middle rack for 5 to 10 minutes, depending how brown you like it. You can put it on a baking sheet or put it straight on the rack. Flip halfway through.

2. Mix the butter and mustard together, and spread it on the toast. Sprinkle with grated cheese.

3. Turn on the oven's broiler and broil for 3 to 5 minutes, until the cheese is nicely toasted and browned.

Friendly Advice: Never walk away from the oven when you have something in the broiler, and check on it frequently, because everything will burn up if you're a minute too late!

"The History of a Squash"

Once upon a time a farmer planted a little seed in his garden, and after a while it sprouted and became a vine, and bore many squashes. One day in October, when they were ripe, he picked one and took it to market. A grocer-man bought and put it in his shop. That same morning, a little girl, in a brown hat and blue dress, with a round face and snub nose, went and bought it for her mother. She lugged it home, cut it up, and boiled it in the big pot; mashed some of it, with salt and butter, for dinner; and to the rest she added a pint of milk, two eggs, four spoons of sugar, nutmeg, and some crackers; put it in a deep dish, and baked it till it was brown and nice; and next day it was eaten by a family named March.

CHAPTER 10: "THE P.C. AND P.O."

The only actual recipe in the novel, Beth's story for *The Pickwick Portfolio* makes a light but homey side dish. If you find the traditional Thanksgiving sweet potatoes with marshmallows to be overly sugary, this would make a nice alternative.

Makes 6 servings

- 2 pounds butternut squash, peeled and cut into 1-inch cubes
- 2 tablespoons kosher salt
- 4 tablespoons butter, divided
- 2 cups whole milk

- 2 eggs
- 4 tablespoons brown sugar, divided
- ½ teaspoon nutmeg, plus a pinch more
- 45 crumbled saltine crackers (about 2 cups crumbs), divided

1. Boil the squash with the salt in a large pot of water until soft, 15 to 20 minutes.

2. Drain the water and mash the squash with 2 tablespoons of the butter.

3. Preheat the oven to 375°F and butter a heatproof dish that holds at least 2 quarts.

4. Whisk the milk and eggs together in a medium bowl and add to the squash.

5. Add 2 tablespoons of the sugar, ½ teaspoon nutmeg, 1 cup cracker crumbs, and more salt if needed.

6. Melt the remaining 2 tablespoons butter, and mix in a small bowl with the remaining 1 cup cracker crumbs, 2 tablespoons sugar, and pinch of nutmeg.

7. Put the squash in the prepared dish and sprinkle the top with the crumb mixture.

8. Bake until heated through and browned on top, 30 to 45 minutes. It should be puffed and slightly set in the middle.

Beth

Dainty
Dishes

The pleasantest room in the house was set apart for Beth, and in it was gathered everything that she most loved,—flowers, pictures, her piano, the little work-table, and the beloved pussies. Father's best books found their way there, mother's easy-chair, Jo's desk, Amy's finest sketches; and every day Meg brought her babies on a loving pilgrimage, to make sunshine for Aunty Beth. John quietly set apart a little sum, that he might enjoy the pleasure of keeping the invalid supplied with the fruit she loved and longed for; old Hannah never wearied of concocting dainty dishes to tempt a capricious appetite, dropping tears as she worked; and from across the sea came little gifts and cheerful letters, seeming to bring breaths of warmth and fragrance from lands that know no winter.

CHAPTER 40: "THE VALLEY OF THE SHADOW"

Most Victorian cookbooks have a chapter on "invalid cookery," or food and remedies for the sick. In this era, home nursing was a woman's domain. In fact, female authority on the subject was a big reason why women were accepted as nurses in the Civil War, at a time when they might have been considered too weak to practice medicine.[6] Louisa May Alcott was a Civil War nurse herself![7]

Hannah, as an experienced cook and nurse, would have an arsenal of foods and beverages to combat illness. The novel doesn't specify what Hannah makes for her patients, other than boiled chicken and beef-tea, so we looked through historical books and picked out our favorite dainty dishes and drinks for you to try.

---

6   Veit, *Food in the Civil War Era*, 24.
7   Carolyn Strom Collins and Christina Wyss Eriksson, *Little Women Treasury* (New York: Viking Penguin, 1996), 8–9.

Modest Chicken

Two easy-chairs stood side by side at the head of the table, in which sat Beth and her father, feasting modestly on chicken and a little fruit.

CHAPTER 22: "PLEASANT MEADOWS"

You might think boiled chicken would be tasteless, but as long as you don't overcook it, it will come out moist and tender, and it's much less messy than roasting it—the only trade-off is that you don't get the crispy skin. It's very nice with drawn butter (page 73). If you like liver, it can be cooked, mashed, and added to the drawn butter sauce.

Makes 2 or 3 servings

- 1 whole chicken
- water
- 2 tablespoons kosher salt

1. Fill a large stockpot with enough water to cover the chicken and add salt. Set it to boil over high heat.

2. Remove the neck and giblets from the cavity of the chicken (save them for broth if you like, or just toss them).

3. When the water boils, put in the chicken and return to a boil. Turn down the heat to medium-low and simmer, covered, for 45 minutes.

4. Remove from heat and let stand until the internal temperature of the chicken has reached 165°F.

5. Take the chicken out and divide it into bone-in pieces or remove all the meat from the bones, depending how you'd like to serve it. It can be served warm with a drawn butter sauce (page 73) or cold in sandwiches or chicken salad.

Friendly Advice: The cooking water can be saved to make broth—after you remove the meat, put the bones, giblets (except the liver), and neck back in the water. Add onion, carrot, and celery, and simmer uncovered until the flavors are concentrated to your taste.

Tidbit of History: Deeply Misguided Victorian Remedies

A lot of the remedies in Victorian cookbooks might be helpful and comforting, but others sound downright disgusting or are flat-out dangerous. Check out these poor choices! And in case it's not obvious—don't try these at home.

⚜

An ointment made from the common ground-worms, which boys dig to bait fishes, rubbed on with the hand, is said to be excellent, when the sinews are drawn up by any disease or accident.

⚜

For a prick with a pin, or a slight cut, nothing will more effectually stop the bleeding than old cobwebs compressed into a lump and applied to the wound, or bound on it with a rag. A scrap of cotton wadding is also good for stopping blood.

Old cobwebs don't sound very hygienic, even if you don't have gauze around.

⚜

Break a fresh egg into a saucer, and mix a little sugar with it; also, if approved, a small quantity of wine. Beat the whole to a strong froth. It is considered a restorative.

⚜

And here's the doozy: *Mix two table-spoonfuls of extract of lead with a bottle of rain or river water. Then add two table-spoonfuls of brandy, and shake it well.* The cookbook even confidently adds the footnote: *These remedies are all very simple; but the author knows them to have been efficacious whenever tried.*

Hot Lemonade

One of the more appealing home remedies of the time period, we imagine Victorians drinking this like we do Emergen-C. It's pleasant, fragrant, and, in its original form, intensely sweet—the original recipe calls for half a cup of sugar! Unless you're trying to soothe a cough, we don't suggest using that much.

- 1 lemon
- 2 tablespoons sugar, or to taste
- 4 cups (1 quart) boiling water

1. Slice the lemon, leaving the rind on.

2. In a large, heatproof bowl, mix the sugar into the lemon, using a spoon, until it becomes pasty. Smash the lemon a little to better release the juice.

3. Pour the boiling water into the mixture and stir until the sugar dissolves.

4. Serve in teacups.

Toast Water

Toast water shows up in cookbooks into the 20th century, including a 1939 *Navy Handbook of the Hospital Corps*! It's surprisingly pleasant to drink.

Makes 2 servings

- 2 slices bread
- 4 cups (1 quart) water

1. Toast the bread until it's browned but not at all burnt on both sides (dry, no butter) and boil the water.

2. Put the toast in a heatproof bowl and pour the boiling water over it.

3. Let stand until it is cool, then drain out the water into a pitcher. Don't squeeze the bread too much or you'll get crumbs.

4. Discard the mushy bread and serve the toast water chilled.

Apple Water

The American Frugal Housewife (1832) cookbook says, "This is given as sustenance when the stomach is too weak to bear broth," but it makes a delightful and refreshing beverage, whatever your state of health.

Makes 2 servings

- 4 cups (1 quart) boiling water
- 2 tart apples, like Granny Smith
- zest of 1 lemon
- ½ tablespoon sugar, or to taste (optional)

1. While the water is boiling, thinly slice the apples (no need to remove skin or core) and place in a large bowl with the lemon zest and sugar, if using.

2. Pour the boiling water over the apples, cover, and let stand until cool.

3. Strain the liquid from of the apples and serve the apple water chilled.

4. Discard the apples or save for another use, like applesauce or apple pancakes.

Beth

CHAPTER 4

Amy

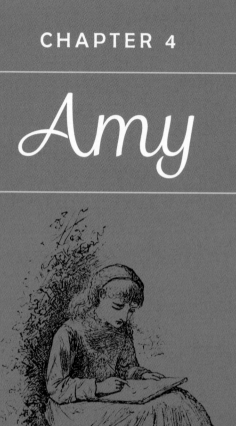

Amy, though the youngest, was a most important person,—in her own opinion at least. A regular snow-maiden, with blue eyes, and yellow hair curling on her shoulders, pale and slender, and always carrying herself like a young lady mindful of her manners.

CHAPTER 1: "PLAYING PILGRIMS"

Amy gets a bad rap. Let this book to be the first to tell you: You don't have to be anti-Amy to be Team Jo. In fact, if you love Jo, you can find plenty to appreciate in the most maligned of March sisters.

When *Little Women* fans and scholars trash poor Amy, they're often talking about who she is as a 12-year-old. Yes, she burns Jo's manuscript, which is egregious, and we might even go so far as to say that Amy deserves that ice-water dunk. But no one should be judged for what they did as a preteen, and Amy has one of the most compelling character arcs in the story, going from the annoying family baby to a practical yet high-minded woman who ends up marrying for love.

Grown-up Amy is the popular girl who always knows what to say and wear, and whose hair is somehow flawless all the time. Not very relatable at first glance, maybe. But we also witness how she *works* to achieve this image. She can't afford to go out and order the latest couture from Parisian fashion houses. Amy paints old boots and hats to make them look like new satin, and she accents a hand-me-down dress with tulle for a ball where she wants to look particularly pretty. Let's not forget too that Amy is a creative and ambitious artist with a burning desire to see the world and prove herself. Her best chance at getting out of her parents' house and going abroad is to make the right connections in society. She knows her own strengths, and as a woman of modest means, she's working to use them to her advantage in a world built for wealthy men.

When it comes to eating and drinking, Amy likes the trendy, the sweet, and the fancy. If Amy were a modern foodie, she would be angling to snag an invite to the celebrity chef bistro that just opened downtown. She might consider the plating and presentation of a dish more important than the taste. She would always want an overly intricate dessert. And she'd have a killer social media account documenting restaurant visits with her influencer friends.

In this chapter, we return to the Victorian era and present some of Amy's favorite treats from the book. In the story, Amy uses food to indulge or impress, and so can you. Here we have the tempting pickled limes that she needed to win status among her schoolmates. There's cake for her sweet tooth. You can also attend the elegant lunch she organizes for snooty fellow art students, and if you're feeling really ambitious, sample a Christmas ball menu from her stay in a hotel in Nice, France.

Delicious Pickled Limes

Next day Amy was rather late at school; but could not resist the temptation of displaying, with pardonable pride, a moist brown-paper parcel, before she consigned it to the inmost recesses of her desk. During the next few minutes the rumor that Amy March had got twenty-four delicious limes (she ate one on the way), and was going to treat circulated through her "set," and the attentions of her friends became quite overwhelming.

CHAPTER 7:
"AMY'S VALLEY OF HUMILIATION"

Pickled limes are probably the most iconic food item in *Little Women*, but most people nowadays don't have any idea what they were like. You might imagine something sweet like marmalade, but in fact they are very salty and sour—similar to the preserved lemon and lime pickles that are still common in Middle Eastern, Indian, and Southeast Asian cooking today. The question is, why would school-age children have been so enamored with them? We theorize that it was an early equivalent of Atomic Fireballs, Warheads, Hot Cheetos, etc.—kids seem to like challenging themselves and each other with super-intense snack foods. Not to mention, they were cheap because they were sent over from the West Indies in big barrels filled with seawater.[8] Not much processing required!

If you don't want to just eat them furtively out of your desk, you can mince the limes and add them to sauces and dressings, or serve as an accompaniment to hearty dishes like Mathematical Mutton Curry (page 18).

---

8   Linda Ziedrich, *The Joy of Pickling* (Quarto Publishing Group, 2016), 100.

Makes 1 dozen

- 2 ounces salt
- 12 small Mexican or Key limes
- 4 cups water

1. Dissolve the salt in the water (this was often described as "brine that will bear an egg" because there's enough salt to make an egg float, and we arrived at this ratio by doing exactly that).

2. Wash the limes well and put them in a large jar with a lid. Add as much brine as will fill the jar, with about ½ inch of space at the top.

3. Close the jar and leave it in a cool cabinet for about five months, turning it over every so often to slosh the brine around. Eventually, the peels will turn tender and translucent, and fade to an olive-green color. (It's unclear how long the limes sat in barrels, but at the three-month mark, ours were terribly bitter. By five months they had mellowed and were quite pleasant.)

4. At this point, the limes should be similar to what Amy had at school. As kids did back then, bite a hole in the top and suck out the pulp, if you dare!

In Another Pickle

We are fairly sure that the above method is the type of lime that Amy would have bought for a penny in a shop, but Eliza Acton's *Modern Cookery for Private Families* had another method for home-pickled limes as follows: Cut a deep cross into the bottom of each lime and pack it with salt. Put the limes into a jar with a bit more salt and leave it to stand on the counter for a week, shaking it once a day. At the end of the week, drain off any brine and rinse off the salt. Replace the limes in the jar and cover with hot white vinegar that you have boiled with a variety of whole spices, such as mustard seeds, cloves, black peppercorns, fresh ginger, dried chiles, or garlic. Add the spices to the jar as well, and let them continue to pickle for twelve months. OR, it says you can achieve the same effect if you cook them overnight in a very low oven. This makes a pickle with an intense and exciting flavor—a little goes a long way! The preserving liquid can also be used as a condiment—one recipe calls it a "lemon catsup."

Amy's
Little
Artistic Fête

"Our drawing class breaks up next week, and before the girls separate for the summer, I want to ask them out here for a day. They are wild to see the river, sketch the broken bridge, and copy some of the things they admire in my book. They have been very kind to me in many ways, and I am grateful, for they are all rich, and I know I am poor, yet they never made any difference."

"Why should they?" and Mrs. March put the question with what the girls called her "Maria Theresa air."

"You know as well as I that it *does* make a difference with nearly every one, so don't ruffle up, like a dear, motherly hen, when your chickens get pecked by smarter birds; the ugly duckling turned out a swan, you know;" and Amy smiled without bitterness, for she possessed a happy temper and hopeful spirit.

Mrs. March laughed, and smoothed down her maternal pride as she asked,—

"Well, my swan, what is your plan?"

"I should like to ask the girls out to lunch next week, to take them [for] a drive to the places they want to see, a row on the river, perhaps, and make a little artistic *fête* for them."

"That looks feasible. What do you want for lunch? Cake, sandwiches, fruit, and coffee will be all that is necessary, I suppose?"

"Oh dear, no! We must have cold tongue and chicken, French chocolate and ice-cream, besides. The girls are used to such things, and I want my lunch to be proper and elegant, though I *do* work for my living."

CHAPTER 26: "ARTISTIC ATTEMPTS"

Oof, we feel bad for Amy in this episode. She wants so badly to fit in with her wealthier art classmates, even while feeling the stinging differences between what she and they can afford. Amy and her family go to huge lengths to offer an afternoon's entertainment that might be considered acceptable by this snootier crowd, and after all that trouble, only one person shows up out of the expected 12! The humiliation! It's a teenager's worst nightmare—the popular friends you're trying to win over don't even bother showing up at the party you threw for them. Poor Amy! But the menu selections for this luncheon are certainly elegant and delicious, so soothe your secondhand embarrassment with some of Amy's favorite delicate fare.

Elegant Roast Chicken

This roast chicken, dredged in flour and basted multiple times in butter, has a rich, crispy crust. The chicken is served with a sauce called drawn butter (not just melted butter as we think of it today). It's one of those recipes that sound bizarre at first but turn out to be surprisingly good.

Makes 3 to 4 servings

- 1 whole roasting chicken, skin on, about 4 pounds
- 1½ teaspoons sea salt
- 2 teaspoons pepper, plus about 1 teaspoon more for the butter
- 6 tablespoons (¾ stick) butter, divided
- ⅓ cup flour, sifted
- drawn butter (recipe on page 73)

1. Preheat the oven to 375°F.

2. Sprinkle the chicken all over, inside and out, with the salt and pepper, rubbing it into the skin.

3. Take 2 tablespoons of butter, coat it in about 1 teaspoon of pepper, and put it in the chicken cavity.

4. Dredge the chicken in the flour, shaking off any extra.

5. Melt the remaining 4 tablespoons butter. Use it to butter the roasting pan a little, then baste the chicken all over with a basting brush.

6. Place the chicken in the pan, breast-up, and put it in the oven.

7. Have the melted butter on hand. Every 20 minutes, take out the chicken, close the oven door, and baste the meat all over with melted butter. Return the chicken to the oven as quickly as possible.

8. Roast 20 minutes for every pound of chicken. Check the internal temperature after an hour of roasting by inserting a meat thermometer through the thickest part of the thigh, avoiding the bone, and check the temperature gauge after 10 seconds. The internal temperature of the thigh should be 165°F.

9. Let the chicken rest for 10 minutes while you make the drawn butter sauce.

10. Carve and serve.

Drawn Butter

Makes 1 cup

- ½ cup whole milk
- ½ cup (1 stick) softened butter
- ½ tablespoon minced fresh parsley
- ½ tablespoon flour

1. Heat the milk in a small saucepan over medium-low heat until just starting to bubble.

2. In a small bowl, mash together the butter, parsley, and flour.

3. Pour the milk over the butter and stir quickly to combine.

4. Return the mixture to the saucepan and bring to a boil over medium heat, stirring constantly, until it starts to foam up.

5. Immediately remove it from the heat and transfer to a warmed serving bowl or gravy boat.

Amy

Proper Cake

> The secret to a beautifully light pound cake is whipping in as much air as possible! It's called a pound cake because originally you used a pound each of butter, sugar, flour, and eggs. This one is scaled down by half.

Makes 1 (9 x 5-inch) loaf

- 8 ounces granulated sugar
- zest of 1 large lemon
- 8 ounces butter
- 4 eggs
- juice of 1 large lemon, divided

- 1¼ teaspoons almond extract, divided
- 8 ounces flour
- pinch of salt
- about 1 cup of powdered sugar, shifted

PREPARE THE CAKE:

1. Have all the ingredients at room temperature—this is important to keep the batter from curdling.

2. Preheat the oven to 350°F and grease a 9 x 5-inch loaf pan.

3. Add sugar to a large bowl (or the bowl of a stand mixer) and zest the lemon into the sugar. Rub the zest and sugar together to release the lemon oils.

4. Cream butter and sugar together with a hand mixer or stand mixer until light and fluffy, about 5 minutes.

5. Add eggs, one at a time, and whip for 3 minutes after adding each one, until the mixture is smooth and light, like whipped cream. After the second egg, add half the lemon juice and 1 teaspoon almond extract. After the last egg, beat for 10 more minutes, stopping occasionally to scrape down the sides. Don't worry if it curdles, just keep whipping!

6. Add 1/3 of the flour along with the salt, and beat for just a few seconds, until combined. Repeat with each remaining third of the flour.

7. Spoon the batter into the loaf pan and bake for about 1 hour, or until the top is golden brown and a skewer inserted into the middle comes out clean. (Baking times can vary a lot, so start checking at 45 minutes, but it might take up to 75.)

8. For the glaze, sift the powdered sugar into a small bowl, then mix in the remaining lemon juice a little at a time till it's the consistency you like. Add ¼ teaspoon almond extract. Drizzle over the cake and allow to set before serving.

Amy

Christmas Ball Supper in Nice

The company assembled in the long *salle à manger*, that evening, was such as one sees nowhere but on the Continent. The hospitable Americans had invited every acquaintance they had in Nice, and, having no prejudice against titles, secured a few to add luster to their Christmas ball. [...]

It was a lively scene, for soon the spirit of the social season took possession of every one, and Christmas merriment made all faces shine, hearts happy, and heels light. The musicians fiddled, tooted, and banged as if they enjoyed it; everybody danced who could, and those who couldn't admired their neighbors with uncommon warmth. The air was dark with Davises, and many Joneses gambolled like a flock of young giraffes. The golden secretary darted through the room like a meteor, with a dashing Frenchwoman, who carpeted the floor with her pink satin train. The Serene Teuton found the supper-table, and was happy, eating steadily through the bill of fare, and dismayed the *garcons* by the ravages he committed.

CHAPTER 37: "NEW IMPRESSIONS"

Amy's social grace and talent for art are rewarded with an extended tour of Europe with wealthy relations. While she's in Nice, she reunites with Laurie, who's still miserable from Jo's rejection. They attend a Christmas ball together, where they both see each other with new eyes—it's the beginning of their romance.

In the March sisters' world, French cuisine is revered as the highest and most distinguished of all. Since the novel doesn't spell out what they eat, we scoured menus from the 1800s to find out what a luxe hotel party might have served back then. Might we suggest this beautiful charlotte, which was a frequently featured dessert?

Charlotte Russe

There are many variations on charlotte russe, but the general idea is a chilled dessert with a creamy filling and a soft crust of ladyfingers. Nowadays, Bavarian cream is usually an egg custard mixed with whipped cream, but in the 19th-century French recipes we consulted, it was simply whipped cream mixed with some sort of flavoring, usually fruit. They used isinglass (fish gelatin!) to help it set. This is a surprisingly easy recipe if you use store-bought ladyfingers, and it looks gorgeous.

Makes 8 servings

For the ladyfingers:
- 1 (500-gram) package of ladyfingers

For the Bavarian cream:
- 1 cup fruit purée (raspberry, peach, passionfruit, anything you like. The more exotic, the better!)
- ¼ to 1 cup sugar (adjust depending on the sweetness of the fruit—only something very tart like passionfruit would need the full amount)
- 1 to 2 teaspoons lemon juice (optional; use this if your fruit isn't very tart or has a dull flavor)
- 1 (¼-ounce) envelope plain powdered gelatin
- 3 cups heavy whipping cream

For assembly:
- fresh fruit, for garnishing

PREPARE THE BAVARIAN CREAM:

1. In a small saucepan, combine the fruit purée and sugar to taste (and lemon juice, if using), then add the gelatin and heat until the gelatin is dissolved. Allow to cool to room temperature.

2. Whip the cream to stiff peaks, then gently fold in the fruit purée.

ASSEMBLE THE CHARLOTTE RUSSE:

1. Lightly oil a springform pan, then line the edges with the most attractive of the ladyfingers, bottom sides pointing in. Use the less attractive ones to line the bottom—you may have to break them up a bit to get good coverage.

2. Spoon half of the Bavarian cream into the pan, and smooth it out nicely.

Amy

3. Add another layer of ladyfingers, if you have some left. You can also add a layer of chopped fruit if it's not too juicy.

4. Add the rest of the Bavarian cream, and smooth it out.

5. Cover with plastic wrap and refrigerate until set, at least 2 hours or overnight.

6. Remove the charlotte russe from the pan and decorate the top with fresh fruit. *Voilà!*

Tidbit of History: Arranging a Ball Buffet

This glorious charlotte russe is just one example of a dessert that Amy and Laurie might have encountered on their romantic evening. Suppers like the one they attended were extravagant productions, with three to five courses. And remember, each course wasn't one, but many dishes!

Here's a lovely supper menu we imagined, inspired by this Christmas ball, consisting of historical dishes Amy and Laurie could have enjoyed this night:

- Quenelles de volaille au consommé (chicken dumplings with clear soup)
- Saumon au beurre de Montpellier (salmon with Montpellier butter)
- Dinde truffée (turkey with truffles)
- Fonds d'artichauts à l'Italienne (Italian-style artichoke hearts)
- Jelée d'orange (orange jelly)
- Charlotte russe

If you have the urge to re-create the whole buffet, the famed chef Urbain Dubois gives detailed instructions for arranging the table in his book, *Cuisine artistique*. (His 1868 feast for the royal court listed no fewer than 47 dishes.) Soup is served first, as the only hot item. The rest of the food is placed symmetrically, with entrées on long platters, alternating with side dishes on round plates. He directs chefs to decorate with plentiful garnishes (like all the truffles you can find), flowers, and ornamental sculptures made of fat. Yes, you read that right; Dubois claims they look as elegant as alabaster. (We'll take his word for it.) According to Dubois, you must never discount the power of fantasy in creating haute cuisine—you must keep innovating because the culinary arts are an infinite, inexhaustible science![9]

9   Urbain Dubois, *Cuisine artistique: études de l'école moderne: Ouvrage en deux parties* (Paris: Librairie E. Dentu, 1872), 21–26.

Tidbit of History: Repast from the Past

A lot of us today expect breakfast in the morning, lunch around noon, and dinner or supper in the evening. While reading *Little Women*, you might have noticed that 19th-century mealtimes, while having familiar names, could mean different expectations from ours. So here's a brief overview of the vocabulary:

Breakfast has been the most consistent in meaning over time; it's traditionally the first meal of the day. The Victorian spread tended to be much heartier than the grab-and-go breakfasts we have now.

Lunch in the Civil War era wasn't the significant midday repast we have today. "Lunch" could mean a quick snack that was easily portable for work or travel, it could indicate a party held for friends, especially among women (like Amy's fête for her art classmates, page 70).

Dinner was the most elaborate and important meal of the day. The time depended on the family's schedule and when they could all gather together—it could be anywhere from midday to early evening. Jo's New York boarding house holds their dinner at 5 o'clock (page 42).

Supper, compared to dinner, was relatively light and less structured, but it also usually offered a selection of hot items, in contrast to lunch and tea. Suppers had a social aspect to them and were often tied to formal evening occasions. (Go to page 76 for Amy's Christmas ball supper in France.)

Tea was the final meal of the day, usually with family and occasional friends. Tea had a simpler menu that you could easily add to, in case of unexpected company. Try Beth's toast for tea (page 56).

CHAPTER 5

Laurie

"Curly black hair; brown skin; big, black eyes; handsome
nose; fine teeth; small hands and feet; taller than I am;
very polite, for a boy, and altogether jolly."

CHAPTER 3: "THE LAURENCE BOY"

Is there anyone more charming than Laurie? The answer is no. Theodore Laurence is the definition of the ideal boy next door. When we first meet Laurie, he is rich in money but starving for affection. While the wealthier crowd look down their noses at the Marches in their genteel poverty, Laurie can't believe his good luck that they've adopted him as one of their own, and he goes out of his way to show his gratitude. Laurie is like a lonely, curly-headed puppy who'd been stuck in a gilded cage and has now finally found his humans—he frolics all over with his tail wagging, and he sticks by the family with unwavering devotion. In return for the Marches' kindness, he tactfully offers luxuries that are usually out of their reach, giving the sisters much-needed breaks from work and worry. Mischievous and full of pranks, he makes an excellent BFF for Jo, and their camaraderie (even with the complication of unrequited feelings) is beautiful to behold.

The dishes that readers associate with Laurie reflect who he is: generous, jolly, and somehow both unpretentious and classy at the same time. In the story, Laurie's meals and snacks give him chances to have fun and further cement the bond he has with the Marches. Before they start hanging out, Laurie sends a fine Christmas supper to the girls after they give away their breakfast. (Well, technically, it was his grandfather, but it was Laurie's idea.) Jo cultivates her budding friendship with Laurie when she visits him with a blanc-mange for his sore throat. In the summer, Laurie installs a post office in the hedge between their houses, through which they exchange gifts, including pickles. And when their squad is in full force, Laurie arranges a glorious summer picnic for them all.

Blanc-Mange for Sore Throats

Presently there came a loud ring, then a decided voice, asking for "Mr. Laurie," and a surprised-looking servant came running up to announce a young lady.

"All right, show her up, it's Miss Jo," said Laurie, going to the door of his little parlor to meet Jo, who appeared, looking rosy and kind and quite at her ease, with a covered dish in one hand and Beth's three kittens in the other.

"Here I am, bag and baggage," she said briskly. "Mother sent her love, and was glad if I could do anything for you. Meg wanted me to bring some of her blanc-mange; she makes it very nicely, and Beth thought her cats would be comforting. I knew you'd laugh at them, but I couldn't refuse, she was so anxious to do something."

It so happened that Beth's funny loan was just the thing; for, in laughing over the kits, Laurie forgot his bashfulness, and grew sociable at once.

"That looks too pretty to eat," he said, smiling with pleasure, as Jo uncovered the dish, and showed the blanc-mange, surrounded by a garland of green leaves, and the scarlet flowers of Amy's pet geranium.

"It isn't anything, only they all felt kindly, and wanted to show it. Tell the girl to put it away for your tea: it's so simple you can eat it; and, being soft, it will slip down without hurting your sore throat."

CHAPTER 5: "BEING NEIGHBORLY"

Here we witness the beginning of Jo's beautiful friendship with Laurie, solidified by the Marches' enthusiastic generosity and Laurie's graciousness as a host.

Blanc-mange is a delicate milk pudding which was served as both a dessert and a food for the sick. It has faded almost entirely from the standard American diet, but it was enormously popular in Victorian times, with cookbooks from the era presenting its many variations.

Makes 2 to 4 servings

- 1 tablespoon powdered gelatin or 4 gelatin sheets
- 2 cups whole milk, divided
- 1 egg, beaten
- 3½ tablespoons sugar
- pinch of salt
- zest of 1 lemon

1. In a small bowl, put the gelatin in ½ cup of the milk for 15 minutes to let it bloom.

2. Add a few inches of water to the bottom of a double boiler—make sure the water doesn't touch the top pot—and bring to a boil. Lower the heat to medium-low, so the water is just at a simmer.

3. In a medium bowl, mix the egg and sugar. Whisk in the remaining 1½ cups milk.

4. Put the egg mixture in the top of the double boiler and heat over the simmering water for 20 to 25 minutes, stirring frequently. Taste it to check that it no longer tastes of raw egg—if it does, it needs more time. Take off the heat.

5. Add the salt, gelatin mixture, and lemon zest, and stir until dissolved.

6. Rinse a mold or bowl that will hold at least 2 cups with water, and then strain the blanc-mange mixture into it through a fine-meshed sieve.

7. Let it set in the fridge for a few hours.

8. When you're ready to unmold the blanc-mange, dip it into a bath of hot water for a few seconds till the edges just begin to melt. Invert onto a plate.

Laurie

Peach Pickles for the P.O.

The P.O. was a capital little institution, and flourished wonderfully, for nearly as many queer things passed through it as through the real [post] office. Tragedies and cravats, poetry and pickles, garden-seeds and long letters, music and gingerbread, rubbers, invitations, scoldings, and puppies. The old gentleman liked the fun, and amused himself by sending odd bundles, mysterious messages, and funny telegrams; and his gardener, who was smitten with Hannah's charms, actually sent a love-letter to Jo's care. How they laughed when the secret came out, never dreaming how many love-letters that little post-office would hold in the years to come.

CHAPTER 10: "THE P.C. AND P.O."

When we think of pickles, we think of cucumbers, but they were just one of the many types of pickles that were eaten in the *Little Women* era—to be honest, they pretty much pickled anything that stood still long enough. These peach pickles are addictively sweet and sour, and easy to make! Look for firm peaches, a little on the unripe side.

Makes about 4 cups

- 3 large peaches
- 4 whole cloves
- 2 cups white or cider vinegar
- ½ cup firmly packed brown sugar

1. Wash the peaches well and rub off any excessive fuzz.

2. Chop them into bite-sized pieces, and put them in jars with the cloves.

3. Combine the vinegar and sugar in a small saucepan and bring to a boil.

4. Pour the vinegar mixture over the peaches and seal the jars.

5. Refrigerate for 3 days, then drain off half the vinegar (don't throw it out—a splash of the vinegar mixed with club soda makes a refreshing drink!) and replace it with water. Refrigerate for another week and your pickles will be ready.

Laurie vs. Professor Bhaer

"Jo" should have remained a literary spinster but so many enthusiastic young ladies wrote to me clamorously demanding that she should marry Laurie, or somebody, that I didn't dare to refuse and out of perversity went and made a funny match for her. I expect vials of wrath to be poured out upon my head, but rather enjoy the prospect. —Louisa May Alcott

The moment Jo hides behind a curtain at a ball and bumps into Laurie is the perfect meet-cute. Their friendship that follows is one for the ages. But when Jo doesn't love Laurie back, it's flabbergasting for us readers. It breaks our hearts because we love Laurie, and we can't imagine how anyone can help feeling otherwise. But this outcome taught us two crucial life lessons:

1. No matter how much you want it, the choice for two people to be together is theirs and no one else's, and

2. You can't make yourself love anyone, no matter how much everyone else wants and expects it, even if you wish you could!

Upon further re-reads, we grudgingly get it. Jo and Laurie wouldn't have enough in common to live happily as a couple for one fundamental reason: Jo needs to struggle. She lives for the fight. Laurie, on the other hand, would want to pave the way for her.

In contrast, Professor Bhaer challenges Jo and sees her true self in a way that Laurie never would. The professor's cozy, untidy, absent-minded ways suit Jo perfectly, and though he isn't swoonily handsome like Laurie, he is "attractive as a genial fire, and people seemed to gather about him as naturally as about a warm hearth." Yes, he is rather snobbish about her sensationalist stories, but at least he takes Jo seriously as a writer!

If Jo had married Laurie, she would've had a tough time finding a purpose as a well-to-do housewife. In the sequels, *Little Men* and *Jo's Boys*, you see how Jo achieves her ideal of a fulfilling, important career as an educator and writer with a complementary, patient partner striving for the same goals alongside her.

Advantage: Team Bhaer.

Christmas Supper from Mr. Laurence

The excitement had hardly subsided, when Hannah appeared, with "Mrs. March's compliments, and would the ladies walk down to supper."

This was a surprise, even to the actors; and when they saw the table, they looked at one another in rapturous amazement. It was like Marmee to get up a little treat for them; but anything so fine as this was unheard-of since the departed days of plenty. There was ice-cream,—actually two dishes of it, pink and white,—and cake and fruit and distracting French bonbons, and, in the middle of the table, four great bouquets of hot-house flowers!

It quite took their breath away; and they stared first at the table and then at their mother, who looked as if she enjoyed it immensely.

"Is it fairies?" asked Amy.

"It's Santa Claus," said Beth.

"Mother did it", and Meg smiled her sweetest, in spite of her gray beard and white eyebrows.

"Aunt March had a good fit and sent the supper," cried Jo, with a sudden inspiration.

"All wrong. Old Mr. Laurence sent it," replied Mrs. March.

"The Laurence boy's grandfather! What in the world put such a thing into his head? We don't know him!" exclaimed Meg.

CHAPTER 2: "A MERRY CHRISTMAS"

Having given up their Christmas breakfast to a poor family, the girls are unexpectedly rewarded with a dainty array of treats after they perform the play they've been rehearsing. It turns out their rich, scary, old neighbor, Mr. Laurence (or possibly his handsome young grandson?) heard about their good deed and sent over a marvelous feast. In their reduced financial circumstances, this is utmost luxury. Two kinds of ice-cream? Flowers in the middle of winter? So fancy!

Pink Ice-Cream (Currant and Lemon)

The original recipe suggests you color it with cochineal, a food dye that's made from insects. While cochineal is still used today in many foods, the currant jelly does a perfectly fine job of making the ice-cream pink. If you want a brighter color, by all means feel free to use any food coloring you like.

Makes 4 to 6 servings

- ½ cup red currant jelly (to make your own, see page 25)
- ¼ cup corn syrup
- juice of 1 small lemon
- 2 cups cream
- few drops of red food coloring (optional)

1. Whisk together the jelly and corn syrup, then whisk in the lemon juice, then the cream. Whisk in the food coloring, if using.

2. Freeze in an ice-cream maker (hand-crank for authenticity, or electric for convenience), then allow to harden in the freezer for at least an hour before serving.

White Ice-Cream (Almond and Rose)

The combination of almond and rose is intriguing and difficult to identify if you're tasting it for the first time. It has a distinctly old-fashioned flavor, lovely but clearly from another era.

Makes 4 to 6 servings

- 1 tablespoon arrowroot powder
- 1 cup milk
- 1 cup cream
- ½ cup sugar
- ¼ teaspoon almond extract
- 2 teaspoons rose water (see Friendly Advice below)

1. Mix the arrowroot in a small dish with enough milk to make a thin paste. Make sure there are no lumps.

2. Heat the remaining milk and cream in a medium saucepan over medium heat until it boils.

3. Stir in the arrowroot and bring it back to a boil.

4. Stir in the sugar, briefly boil again, and remove from the heat.

5. Refrigerate the mixture overnight, or until it's entirely cold.

6. Add the almond extract and rose water, and freeze using an ice-cream maker (hand-crank for authenticity, or electric for convenience).

7. Transfer into a storage container and freeze until firm.

Friendly Advice: Look for Ahmed brand rose water, which has a gentle rose scent and isn't strongly perfumed. If you use another brand such as Cortas or Sadaf, start with ¼ teaspoon and add more if you like. The almond and rose flavors should balance each other, as if combining to make a third flavor.

Fine Cake

This is based on a recipe called Federal Cake, which some say goes back to Alexander Hamilton's Federalist political party. They were often cut into small diamond-shaped cakes, but this one is more like a pound cake loaf—old-fashioned and rich, just like Mr. Laurence. Use any kind of raisins you like, or other chopped dried fruit. Dried apricots are especially good here.

Makes 8 servings

- ¼ cup brandy, apple cider, or some other liquid if you prefer
- 8 ounces (1½ cups) raisins
- 8 ounces butter
- 8 ounces (1 cup) sugar
- ½ teaspoon freshly grated nutmeg
- 2 eggs
- ½ teaspoon baking soda
- ½ cup sour cream
- 8 ounces (2¼ cups) flour

1. Have all the ingredients at room temperature.

2. Preheat oven to 375°F and grease a 9 x 5-inch loaf pan with butter or nonstick spray.

3. Combine the brandy or other liquid and raisins in a small bowl and set aside.

4. Cream the butter, sugar, and nutmeg together with a hand mixer or stand mixer.

5. Add the eggs and beat on medium to high speed for 3 to 5 minutes, until it is fluffy and light-colored.

6. Stir the baking soda into the sour cream and beat in.

7. Drain the brandy from the raisins and add the brandy to the mixture.

8. Add the flour in four parts, mixing just until incorporated. Make sure to scrape down the sides of the bowl as you mix.

9. When you get to the last part of the flour, toss the raisins in the flour and add them along with it.

10. Spoon batter into the prepared pan and bake until a toothpick inserted in the middle of the cake comes out clean. Baking time can vary widely depending on the pan and your oven—start testing at 45 minutes but it can take as long as 90 minutes. If you notice the top browning before it's set in the middle, cover with foil and keep baking.

Jolly Picnic Lunch at Camp Laurence

Dear Jo, What ho!

Some English girls and boys are coming to see me to-morrow and I want to have a jolly time. If it's fine, I'm going to pitch my tent in Longmeadow, and row up the whole crew to lunch and croquet,—have a fire, make messes, gypsy fashion, and all sorts of larks. They are nice people, and like such things. Brooke will go, to keep us boys steady, and Kate Vaughn will play propriety for the girls. I want you all to come; can't let Beth off at any price, and nobody shall worry her. Don't bother about rations,—I'll see to that and everything else,—only do come, there's a good fellow!

In a tearing hurry,

Yours ever, LAURIE.

CHAPTER 12: "CAMP LAURENCE"

Laurie has guests visiting from England, so he decides to invite everyone for a big outdoor picnic! Unladylike Jo and Laurie's boorish friend Fred Vaughn do not make a good impression on each other, and things are a little tense until Laurie breaks out the picnic lunch. It's always a little awkward introducing your different friend groups to each other—you never know who's going to show up in a ridiculous hat or who's going to cheat at croquet—but if you bring lots of good food, everything will probably work out okay in the end.

Since the book doesn't specify what they ate at the picnic (other than berries and cream, which Laurie of course takes as an opportunity to tease Jo about her disastrous dinner party (page 34), we chose a variety of picnic fare that sounded delicious and portable. This meal turned out to be one of our favorites, with big pillowy potato rolls, potted ham (we'd never tried it before but it turns out to be amazing), and a crisp cucumber salad. We'd also add the peach pickles (page 86) and pound cake (page 74) to round out the meal.

Hearty Potato Rolls

Why add mashed potatoes to bread? They give it a softer, fluffier texture, a slightly sweet flavor, and help keep it from going stale as quickly. These rolls make excellent sandwiches and would be perfect for hamburger buns (although hamburgers weren't invented until the 1880s).

Makes 16 large rolls

- 2 medium russet potatoes (about 2 cups mashed)
- 1 tablespoon butter
- 1 tablespoon salt
- 2 egg yolks
- 1½ cups milk, warmed, plus more for glazing
- 1 packet active dry yeast (2¼ teaspoons)
- about 6½ cups flour

1. Boil the potatoes, skins on, until they are soft all the way through and the skins are beginning to split.

2. Drain the water and return the potatoes to the pot. Let them sit with the lid on for 15 minutes to an hour (whenever you get back to them), which lets them absorb any extra water and become fluffier.

3. Remove the skins and mash the potatoes in a large bowl with the butter and salt. Make sure they are very smooth, with no lumps.

4. Mix in the egg yolks.

5. Mix in the warm milk and yeast. Let it sit until you see the yeast starting to bubble.

6. Gradually knead in the flour, until the dough is smooth. The amount of flour you need may vary a bit depending on how moist your potatoes are. The dough will be fairly soft, but you should be able to stretch an edge of the dough until it's translucent without tearing (this is called the "windowpane test").

7. Oil the bowl and put the dough back in. Allow to rise until doubled in volume, about 1 hour in a warm place (75°F is ideal) or overnight in the refrigerator.

8. Punch down the dough and divide it into 16 pieces.

9. Form each piece into a tight ball (smooth on top and tucked in tightly underneath) and place them on two parchment-covered sheet pans, about 1 inch apart.

10. Cover with oiled plastic wrap and let rise in a warm place for about an hour, or until doubled in size. They should now be touching each other a bit.

11. Preheat the oven to 350°F.

12. Brush the tops of the rolls with milk.

13. Bake for 20 to 25 minutes, until golden brown and about 200°F to 205°F internally.

Laurie

Potted Ham

Potted ham isn't common in the U.S. anymore, and it's too bad because it's wonderful. It makes a great sandwich spread, or you could serve it as an hors d'oeuvre with crackers. A Victorian cookbook advises, "A jar of this will be found useful to travellers in remote places"—perfect for an outing to Camp Laurence! If you want to be extra-authentic, you'd seal the top of each container with melted lard instead of butter, but really the butter is better.

Makes 6 to 8 servings

- 8 ounces cooked uncured dinner ham, with any gristle, sinew, or chunks of fat discarded
- 7 tablespoons plus 6 tablespoons unsalted butter, divided
- ¼ teaspoon cayenne pepper
- ⅛ teaspoon ground mace
- ⅛ teaspoon nutmeg

1. Chop the ham into 1-inch cubes or smaller.

2. In a small saucepan, melt 7 tablespoons of the butter.

3. Put the ham in a food processor, along with the cayenne pepper, mace, nutmeg, and the melted butter. Blend until mostly smooth, but not totally pasty. The ham should have a finely minced texture. Pack the ham into 3 (½-cup) ramekins.

4. In a small saucepan, melt the remaining 6 tablespoons butter and top each ramekin with 2 tablespoons of it.

5. Cover and refrigerate just until the butter is solid, and then serve.

6. To freeze, cover in plastic wrap, and the potted ham will keep up to 3 months. Defrost overnight in the fridge, then let it come up to room temperature before serving.

Friendly Advice: For a special occasion, try making a batch with cooked chicken breast.

Wholesome Cucumbers

A refreshing, simple salad, perfect as a light summer side.

Makes 3 servings

- 1 English cucumber
- 1 tablespoon apple cider vinegar
- salt and pepper

1. Peel and slice the cucumber very thin. Put the slices in fresh cold water to crisp them.

2. Once you are ready to eat, drain the cucumbers, put them in a dish, and mix with the vinegar.

3. Sprinkle with salt and pepper to taste, and serve.

Get the Receipt

Victorians' produce choices might have been limited during certain seasons, but when they did have vegetables, they could be much fresher than what we're used to. Check out the original recipe for these cucumbers from Mrs. Cornelius:

Cucumbers should be gathered while dew is yet on them, and put immediately into water. Half an hour before dinner, pare and slice them very thin, and let them lie in fresh water till dinner is ready; then drain them, lay them into a dish, sprinkle them with salt, pour on the vinegar, and add the pepper last.

Laurie

CHAPTER 6

The March Family

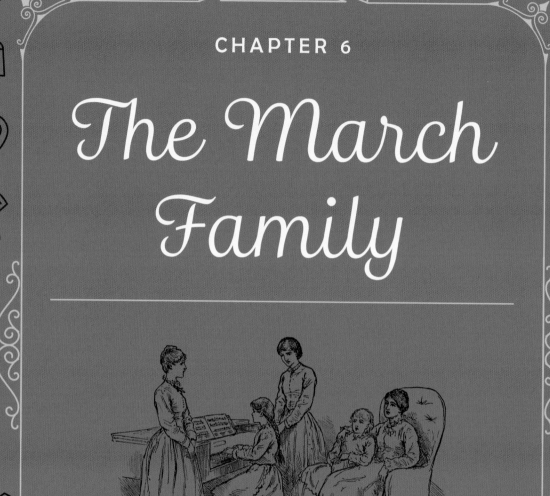

"We can't give up our girls for a dozen fortunes. Rich or poor,
we will keep together and be happy in one another."

Chapter 4: "Burdens"

When we read Little Women, we're all Laurie, peering through a window into the Marches' snug homelife and wishing for a spot by their fireplace. Their household is one of the coziest in all fiction, and the Marches show us how much power there is to a close-knit family. They aren't perfect; each individual member has faults and flaws, and they have their share of spats and sadness. But they all complement and learn from each other, and together they create an enviable place of warmth and support. Also, the Marches stick to their strong beliefs, even if their views aren't fashionable. All their moralizing can admittedly become a bit much sometimes, but they sure don't lack conviction! And watching them encourages us readers to fearlessly champion our ideas and principles, whether they're trendy or not.

March family meals are about togetherness and charity. Hannah's home cooking takes center stage on the dinner table, full of love and consideration for the people she devotedly serves. In the beginning of *Little Women*, the girls are reminded of their good fortune when they give their breakfast to neighbors on Christmas Day; and the book ends with a celebratory apple-picking holiday for Marmee's 60th birthday, with family and friends reflecting on the joys and sorrows they've had over the years. Their feasts are displays of gratitude, especially after long stretches of being apart, and they easily draw lonely outsiders into their comfortable circle.

Hannah's Plain Wholesome Vittles

DEAR MIS MARCH,—

I jes drop a line to say we git on fust rate. The girls is clever and fly round right smart. Miss Meg is going to make a proper good housekeeper; she hes the liking for it, and gits the hang of things surprisin quick. Jo doos beat all for goin ahead, but she don't stop to cal'k'late fust, and you never know where she's like to bring up. She done out a tub of clothes on Monday, but she starched 'em afore they was wrenched, and blued a pink calico dress till I thought I should a died a laughin. Beth is the best of little creeters, and a sight of help to me, bein so forehanded and dependable. She tries to learn everything, and really goes to market beyond her years; likewise keeps accounts, with my help, quite wonderful. We have got on very economical so fur; I don't let the girls hev coffee only once a week, accordin to your wish, and keep em on plain wholesome vittles. Amy does well about frettin, wearin her best clothes and eatin sweet stuff. Mr. Laurie is as full of didoes as usual, and turns the house upside down frequent; but he heartens up the girls, and so I let em hev full swing. The old gentleman sends heaps of things, and is rather wearin, but means wal, and it aint my place to say nothin. My bread is riz, so no more at this time. I send my duty to Mr. March, and hope he's seen the last of his Pewmonia.

"Yours Respectful,

"HANNAH MULLET."

CHAPTER 16: "LETTERS"

Hannah has been with the family since Meg was a baby, and she is "more a friend than a servant." She's worked for the Marches since before they lost their money but, faithful creature that she is, decides to stick with them. Hannah takes care of most of the housework and cooking, which is backbreaking labor in these times. She stays in the background of the story, but if we're talking about the Marches' meals, she is the star of the production. Hannah cares deeply for the sisters, and she bakes their daily bread with great affection. Fiercely protective, she looks after the girls in their parents' absence, making sure to keep them on "plain wholesome vittles."

Hot Turn-Overs, or "Muffs"

There was a momentary lull, broken by Hannah, who stalked in, laid two hot turn-overs on the table, and stalked out again. These turn-overs were an institution; and the girls called them "muffs," for they had no others, and found the hot pies very comforting to their hands on cold mornings.

Hannah never forgot to make them, no matter how busy or grumpy she might be, for the walk was long and bleak; the poor things got no other lunch and were seldom home before two.

CHAPTER 4: "BURDENS"

In Victorian times, ladies would carry around a muff, a cylinder of fur to warm their hands on cold winter days. Since the sisters don't have any, Hannah makes them hot turn-overs—both as a convenient, portable snack and to keep their hands warm. Aw, Hannah can be a grouch sometimes, but she's a soft-hearted sweetie who's always looking out for you. She probably uses a simple crust that's not too flaky or buttery, and rolls it out thick to keep the "muffs" from crumbling in pockets. Turn-overs were often fried back then, but Hannah would bake hers, since she wouldn't want to stain the girls' clothes!

Makes 8 turn-overs

- 3 tart apples, like Granny Smith
- 4 or 5 tablespoons water
- 2 or 3 tablespoons packed brown sugar
- scant ½ teaspoon nutmeg
- 1 tablespoon butter
- 1 Double Pie Crust (page 50)
- extra flour for rolling

1. Core and peel the apples, and slice them small and thin.

2. Heat a very large skillet over high heat until hot, then lower to medium-high. Put in the water, and then the apples. Cook for about 4 minutes, or until some of the apples are limp, but others are still a bit stiff.

3. Add the brown sugar and nutmeg. Cook for 2 more minutes, mixing occasionally with a wooden spoon.

4. Add the butter, mix, and cook 1 more minute. Take off the heat and set aside.

5. Preheat the oven to 400°F.

6. Flour a large, clean surface and your rolling pin. Roll out the pie dough, repairing any cracks by pressing them together, until it's ¼ inch thick. Cut into 4 x 4-inch squares. Scoop about 2 tablespoons stewed apple into the center of each square, and then fold them from corner to corner into a triangle, pressing and crimping the edges together with a fork. (If you find the dough hard to manage, folding in half into rectangles is easier, although the result might not be as cute.)

7. Place the turn-overs on a baking sheet 1 inch apart. Poke a few holes into each turn-over with a fork or knife. Optional: Hannah probably wouldn't have done this, but the turn-overs are even nicer if you brush the tops with milk and sprinkle them with sugar before baking.

8. Bake for 15 minutes in the preheated oven until the edges are browned. Lower the temperature to 350°F and bake for another 5 minutes.

Friendly Advice: Your sliced apples should have enough room that you can mix them easily in the skillet. If you don't have a very large skillet and your apples are overcrowded, split the batch into two skillets over two burners. If you have any leftover pie crust, make pie crust cookies! Roll out the dough, cut into shapes of your choice, sprinkle with sugar and preferred spices, and bake for 8 to 10 minutes at 350°F.

Cale-Cannon

[Mr. Davis] did not soon forget the reproachful glance Amy gave him, as she went, without a word to any one, straight into the ante-room, snatched her things, and left the place "forever," as she passionately declared to herself. She was in a sad state when she got home; and when the older girls arrived, some time later, an indignation meeting was held at once. Mrs. March did not say much, but looked disturbed, and comforted her afflicted little daughter in her tenderest manner. Meg bathed the insulted hand with glycerine and tears; Beth felt that even her beloved kittens would fail as a balm for griefs like this; Jo wrathfully proposed that Mr. Davis be arrested without delay; and Hannah shook her fist at the "villain," and pounded potatoes for dinner as if she had him under her pestle.

CHAPTER 7: "AMY'S VALLEY OF HUMILIATION"

In the late 1840s, there were large numbers of Irish women fleeing from the Great Famine to the U.S. There are theories that Hannah is Irish, although the evidence is inconclusive. Irish servants had a huge influence on Victorian American cookery. In middle-class kitchens, they avoided plain potatoes and preferred to serve dishes like this cale-cannon (more commonly known as colcannon).[10]

Makes 6 servings

- ½ head of cabbage, about 1½ pounds
- ¼ cup kosher salt, divided, plus more for seasoning
- 3 pounds russet potatoes, peeled and halved
- ½ cup (1 stick) butter, melted
- 1 teaspoon pepper, or to taste

---

10   Veit, *Food in the Civil War Era*, 12–14.

1. Core and cut the cabbage into four pieces. Separate the leaves.

2. In a large pot, starting in cold water with about 2 tablespoons of salt, boil the cabbage leaves for 10 to 15 minutes.

3. In a second large pot, starting in cold water with about 2 tablespoons of salt, boil the potatoes for 20 to 25 minutes.

4. Drain the cabbage and squeeze out excess water, then mince it very small.

5. Drain and mash the potatoes, then gradually mix in cabbage, butter, pepper, and 1 teaspoon salt, or to taste.

Friendly Advice: If the potatoes seem too dry, add a little warm milk.

The March Family

Good Family Bread

My bread is riz, so no more at this time. I send my duty to Mr. March, and hope he's seen the last of his Pewmonia.

CHAPTER 16: "LETTERS"

A basic bread recipe would have been the cornerstone of any cook's repertoire, and the original text from Mrs. Cornelius is full of digressions about the moral superiority of baking your own bread. This makes a hearty white loaf, perfect for sandwiches, bread-pudding, or that weird asparagus toast dish on page 41 (trust us, it's really good!). You can easily double this recipe if you like.

Makes 1 loaf

For the sponge:
- 3 tablespoons cornmeal
- 1 teaspoon kosher salt
- 1½ cups water
- ½ cup milk
- ½ teaspoon active dry yeast
- 1 cup flour (5 ounces)

For the bread:
- 3 cups flour (15 ounces), plus a bit more for kneading
- 1 tablespoon kosher salt
- about 2 teaspoons olive oil or vegetable oil for greasing
- milk, for brushing

PREPARE THE SPONGE:

1. The night before you want to bake the bread, boil the cornmeal, salt, and water in a small pot over medium heat until the cornmeal is softened and the mixture thickens, 3 to 5 minutes.

2. Stir in the milk and allow to cool to room temperature.

3. Transfer to a large bowl, and mix in the yeast and flour. Cover and let stand overnight in a warm place (about 75°F is ideal). This is your sponge.

PREPARE THE BREAD:

1. The next day, add the 3 cups flour to the sponge and mix well. Cover and let it rest 30 minutes.

2. Add the kosher salt.

3. Knead the dough by hand or in a stand mixer until it feels silky and not too sticky. You should be able to stretch an edge of the dough until it's translucent without tearing (this is called the "windowpane test"). This should take 10 to 15 minutes. As you knead, add flour as needed, but not so much that the dough becomes stiff.

4. Oil the bowl you were using (no need to wash it) and put the dough in, turning it to coat.

5. Cover and let rise for 1 hour in a warm place.

6. Grease a 9 x 5-inch loaf pan with oil.

7. Once the dough has grown puffy (if you poke it, it should stay poked and not spring back) and has nearly doubled in size, gently punch it down.

8. Remove the dough from the bowl and place it on a floured surface. Spread it out in a more or less rectangular shape, and press out any large bubbles. Roll it tightly lengthwise. Flip the loaf over so the seam is on the bottom, and tuck the long ends underneath so you have a tight loaf shape. Place it in the greased loaf pan, seam-side down.

9. Cover the dough with a damp towel or oiled plastic wrap and let rise for 1 hour, or until puffy and nearly doubled in size.

10. Preheat the oven to 375°F.

11. Brush the top of the loaf with milk. Make a deep slash along the top with a serrated knife, and immediately put it in the oven.

12. Bake 30 to 45 minutes, or until the loaf is browned and the internal temperature rises above 190°F; 200°F to 205°F is usually when the crust will be nicely browned.

13. Remove the loaf from the pan immediately and lay it on its side to cool.

Friendly Advice: If you prefer a tender crust, wrap the loaf in a towel while cooling and the steam will soften it.

The March Family

Christmas Breakfast from the Engel-Kinder

"Merry Christmas, little daughters! I'm glad you began at once, and hope you will keep on. But I want to say one word before we sit down. Not far away from here lies a poor woman with a little new-born baby. Six children are huddled into one bed to keep from freezing, for they have no fire. There is nothing to eat over there; and the oldest boy came to tell me they were suffering hunger and cold. My girls, will you give them your breakfast as a Christmas present?"

They were all unusually hungry, having waited nearly an hour, and for a minute no one spoke; only a minute, for Jo exclaimed impetuously,—"I'm so glad you came before we began!"

Chapter 2: "A Merry Christmas"

A letter from their father has just reminded Meg, Jo, Beth, and Amy to be more selfless, and they promise to try with tears in their eyes. Their resolve is tested on Christmas morning when Marmee suggests that they give away their special holiday breakfast. After the briefest hesitation (where we imagine they're taking a moment to mourn their rare treats), the sisters pack up the meal with admirable enthusiasm, especially considering they've already been waiting to eat for an hour and are probably getting pretty hangry. The Marches deliver their presents to the Hummels, an impoverished German family living in a freezing room with no food or heat. In their gratitude, the little Hummel children call them *Engel-kinder*, or "angel children," and the sisters are reminded of how lucky they are. This scene pushes us readers to remember that we don't need to have everything to donate something, and that Christmas should be a day to give rather than receive.

Buckwheat Cakes

Meg was already covering the buckwheats, and piling the bread into one big plate.

CHAPTER 2: "A MERRY CHRISTMAS"

> Mrs. Cornelius has a variety of methods for buckwheat cakes, including one that uses only buckwheat flour, buttermilk, and baking soda. That version isn't bad at all, but the addition of an egg makes for a much lighter, fluffier pancake.

Makes about 12 small cakes

- 1 cup buckwheat flour
- ½ teaspoon baking soda
- ¼ teaspoon kosher salt
- 1 tablespoon sugar
- 1 egg
- 1 cup buttermilk
- butter, for the pan, plus more for serving
- maple syrup, for serving

1. Preheat a frying pan over medium-low heat.

2. Whisk the flour, baking soda, salt, and sugar together in a medium bowl.

3. In a small bowl, beat the egg into the buttermilk, then pour over dry ingredients and whisk until mixed. It will be rather thick compared to regular pancake batter.

4. Melt the butter in the hot pan and drop in spoonfuls of batter.

5. Cook until bubbles start to form, 2 or 3 minutes for small (2 to 3-inch diameter) cakes. They will cook rather quickly, so pay attention!

6. Flip over and cook about another minute—you will see the cakes puff up slightly.

7. Serve with butter and maple syrup.

Amy's Muffins

"I shall take the cream and the muffins," added Amy, heroically giving up the articles she most liked.

CHAPTER 2: "A MERRY CHRISTMAS"

> These are what we think of as English muffins, not the sweet cakey kind. They are delicious right out of the pan, but even better toasted. It's not surprising that they would be Amy's favorite!

Makes about 12 muffins

- 2 cups milk
- 1 tablespoon butter
- 1 packet active dry yeast (2¼ teaspoons)
- 1 egg
- 2½ cups flour
- 1½ teaspoons kosher salt
- jelly and butter, or clotted cream, for serving

1. In a small saucepan over medium heat, warm the milk and butter together just until the butter begins to melt. Don't let it get too hot—if you dip your finger in, it shouldn't be uncomfortable.

2. Transfer the milk mixture to a large bowl. Stir until the butter is completely melted, then add the yeast.

3. Let sit in a warm place until the yeast dissolves, about 5 minutes.

4. Meanwhile, beat the egg with a fork in a small bowl until foamy.

5. Stir the egg into the milk, then add in the flour and salt gradually—it will be a thick batter.

6. Cover and set in a warm place to rise for 45 minutes to 1 hour. It should approximately double in size.

7. Once the batter is ready, heat a large nonstick frying pan or griddle over medium heat. Have the lid ready nearby.

8. Generously grease the insides of 4 English muffin rings with butter or nonstick spray and place them in the pan.

9. Give the batter a gentle stir to break up the bubbles a bit, then spoon some batter into each ring. For 3½-inch rings, use a bit less than half a cup of batter—you may need to adjust if your rings are a different size.

10. Turn the heat down to medium-low.

11. Put the lid on the pan and let cook for 5 minutes, or until the muffins are golden brown on the bottom. You should see bubbles rising up, and the top of the muffin should be set, not liquid.

12. Pull off the rings if they'll come easily (if not, leave them on), and flip the muffins over.

13. Put the lid back on and cook for another 3 to 5 minutes, until browned on the other side. Remove from pan.

14. Turn the heat back up to medium, re-grease the rings, and repeat with the remaining batter.

15. Let the muffins cool a bit, then split them carefully with a fork. Serve with jelly and butter or clotted cream.

Friendly Advice: These freeze well and are so much better than store-bought that it's worth making a big batch. When you cut them in half, use a fork to split them apart rather than a knife—it maximizes the "nooks and crannies" that crisp up when you toast them.

Comforting Gruel

Mrs. March gave the mother tea and gruel, and comforted her with promises of help, while she dressed the little baby as tenderly as if it had been her own.

CHAPTER 2: "A MERRY CHRISTMAS"

From the way gruel is often described in fiction, as something freezing peasants or jailed criminals have to survive on, we expected this to be terrible. However, it's actually very tasty, like a thinner, drinkable oatmeal. Perfect for a breakfast on the go, or for someone in bed with a cold.

Makes 1 serving

- ¼ cup rolled oats
- 2⅓ cups cold water, divided
- small handful of raisins (optional)
- ¼ teaspoon kosher salt
- 2 teaspoons brown sugar
- ⅛ teaspoon freshly grated nutmeg

1. Grind the rolled oats in a food processor until they're about the consistency of coarse cornmeal.

2. Mix the ground oats with ⅓ cup cold water in a small bowl or mug and stir well. Set aside.

3. Bring the remaining 2 cups water to a boil in a medium skillet.

4. Add the soaked oatmeal and stir well. Add a handful of raisins if desired and let it all boil over medium heat for 8 to 10 minutes, until thickened but still liquid. Keep stirring to keep it from clumping.

5. Transfer the gruel back to the small bowl or mug. Add the salt, brown sugar, and nutmeg (adjust flavors as you like) and serve.

Apple-Picking Holiday

There were a great many holidays at Plumfield, and one of the most delightful was the yearly apple-picking; for then the Marches, Laurences, Brookes, and Bhaers turned out in full force and made a day of it. [...]

Then Jo and Meg, with a detachment of the bigger boys, set forth the supper on the grass, for an out-of-door tea was always the crowning joy of the day. The land literally flowed with milk and honey on such occasions, for the lads were not required to sit at table, but allowed to partake of refreshment as they liked,—freedom being the sauce best beloved by the boyish soul. They availed themselves of the rare privilege to the fullest extent, for some tried the pleasing experiment of drinking milk while standing on their heads, others lent a charm to leap-frog by eating pie in the pauses of the game, cookies were sown broadcast over the field, and apple turn-overs roosted in the trees like a new style of bird. The little girls had a private tea-party, and Ted roved among the edibles at his own sweet will.

CHAPTER 47: "HARVEST TIME"

Phew, we can all relax! We are at the novel's epilogue, which shows us that the Marches are living happily ever after. Nothing is perfect, of course. Beth's absence will forever be a hole in their hearts, and her namesake, Amy and Laurie's daughter, is sickly and might not live long. (Spoiler from the sequels: She does live and grows up to be lovely.) But despite their sadness, the sisters are at the center of a contented, joyful, flourishing family, and they have chosen paths of love and fulfillment.

It's especially satisfying to see that Jo has found her purpose in the school she's started with Professor Bhaer. She's happy to have this huge project for all that restless energy she's had pent up all her life. By establishing and leading a house full of boys, she's also created a place for herself where she won't be as hampered by society's limited expectations for women. Not having to be ladylike all the time? What freedom that is for Jo!

The family remains as close as ever, starting new traditions, like this annual harvest holiday to celebrate their crop of apples and kids. This year, they celebrate Marmee's 60th birthday with a glorious outdoor tea. And so, we close this cookbook as the novel does, with apple turn-overs (page 104), pie, cookies, and tea *al fresco*.

Charming Ham Pie for Leapfrog

A cold meat pie could be made ahead for a holiday and then readily cut into slices to carry around—no wonder it was such a popular choice for outdoor picnics. Not to mention, it looks impressive with lots of decorations on the crust and feeds a ton of people, so it's an excellent party dish.

Makes 1 (9-inch) pie

For the hot water crust:
- 6 tablespoons lard, diced
- 6 tablespoons butter, diced
- 1 scant cup water
- 5 cups flour
- 1½ teaspoons kosher salt
- 2 beaten eggs plus another one for brushing the crust

For the pie filling:
- 3 tablespoons butter
- 1 pound white mushrooms, thinly sliced
- 1 small onion, diced
- 2 sprigs plus 1 teaspoon fresh thyme leaves, divided
- ¾ tablespoon plus a pinch of kosher salt, divided

- pepper
- 2 pounds diced ham
- 2 tablespoons chopped fresh parsley, divided
- 1 teaspoon chopped fresh sage
- ¼ teaspoon ground allspice
- 3 large boneless chicken breasts, diced into ½-inch cubes
- ½ teaspoon ground mace
- zest of 1 lemon
- 6 eggs, hard-boiled, peeled, and left whole

For the jellied stock:
- 1 tablespoon powdered gelatin
- ¼ cup water
- 1 cup chicken stock
- mustard, for serving

PREPARE THE HOT WATER CRUST:

1. Put the lard, butter, and water in a medium saucepan and gently warm over low heat until melted; do not let it boil.

2. Stir together the flour and salt in a large bowl. Make a hollow in the center and add the two beaten eggs, stirring them gently around with a knife so they are half mixed with the flour.

3. Pour in the melted fat and water and mix together to form a soft dough; add up to 3 tablespoons extra warm water if it is too dry. Knead gently, adding more flour if it is too sticky to handle.

4. Wrap the dough in plastic wrap and refrigerate until cold, at least 1 hour.

PREPARE THE PIE FILLING:

1. Heat the butter in a medium skillet over medium-high heat.

2. Add the mushrooms and onion, and sauté with the sprigs of thyme, a pinch of salt, and lots of pepper.

3. In a large bowl, mix the cold ham with 1 tablespoon parsley and the sage, allspice, and pepper to taste. In another large bowl, mix the diced chicken with ¾ tablespoons salt, the remaining 1 tablespoon parsley, 1 teaspoon fresh thyme, and the mace, lemon zest, and pepper to taste.

ASSEMBLE AND BAKE THE PIE:

1. Preheat oven to 350°F. Grease a 9 x 3-inch round pan with a removable bottom with butter.

2. Cut off a generous quarter of the pastry and keep in the fridge, for the lid.

3. On a floured surface, roll out the rest of the pastry into a 13 to 14-inch circle, about ⅓-inch thick.

4. Use this to line the cake pan, pressing the pastry into the sides and flattening any overlap with your fingers. It should come 2½ to 3 inches up the sides of the pan.

5. Put half of the ham at the bottom of the pie, then the chicken, then the whole boiled eggs, the mushrooms and onions, and finally another layer of ham. Mound

it up a little so that the top of the pie is convex rather than concave.

6. Roll out the reserved piece of pastry into a circle about the size of the pan. Brush the edges of the lining pastry with a little of the remaining beaten egg (you'll need the rest later), and lay the pastry lid on top of the pie. Crimp the edges so they are sealed inside the pan—don't crimp them onto the edge of the pan as you usually would for a pie, because doing so will keep you from removing it nicely from the pan.

7. Cut a 2-inch diameter hole in the center of the pastry lid. Make a coil rim with extra pastry around the edge of the hole. This will help keep the liquid inside from bubbling out as it cooks.

8. Decorate the top of the pie with extra pastry, as you choose—you can make leaves, flowers, stars, or letters.

9. Bake for 30 minutes. Reduce the temperature to 325°F and bake for 1 hour and 15 minutes more. If the top crust is concave instead of convex, a pool of juice and fat may form around the center hole during baking that you'll want to remove with a turkey baster, or the crust may become soggy.

10. Remove the pie from the oven and carefully release it from the pan.

11. Brush the top and sides of the pie with beaten egg and cook for another 15 minutes to set the glaze.

PREPARE THE JELLIED STOCK AND SERVE:

1. Take the pie out of the oven and allow to cool completely.

2. Meanwhile, put the powdered gelatin in the ¼ cup water and let it sit for 10 minutes. Whisk into the chicken stock.

3. Heat the stock in a small pan over low heat until it's just pourable—not too hot.

4. Pour the jellied stock slowly into the center hole in the pie. The filling will have shrunk, creating a space around the edge that is traditionally filled with jellied stock. Refrigerate to let the gelatin set.

5. Serve the pie cold or at room temperature, in slices with mustard.

Cookies to Eat in a Field

Simple sugar cookies, flavored with nutmeg. You could use pre-ground nutmeg for this, but freshly grated is recommended. These are very nice dipped in milk, as the Plumfield boys would have done for the outdoor harvest supper.

Makes 2 dozen (2½-inch) cookies

- 1¾ cups flour
- heaping ½ teaspoon baking soda
- ½ whole nutmeg, grated or 1½ teaspoons ground nutmeg
- ¼ cup white sugar
- ½ cup brown sugar
- ½ cup butter
- 1 large egg
- ¼ cup heavy cream

1. Mix the flour and baking soda together in a medium bowl. Grate the nutmeg into the bowl, and sift together. Set aside.

2. In a large bowl, beat the white sugar, brown sugar, and butter until light and fluffy.

3. In a small bowl, beat the egg and add the cream to it. Add the egg mixture gradually to the butter and sugar, then beat.

4. Gradually add the dry ingredients into the wet until well mixed. Add a little extra flour at a time if it's too sticky to handle, but the softer the dough, the better the cookie will be.

5. Wrap the dough and refrigerate for 2 hours until firm.

6. Preheat the oven to 375°F and line baking sheets with parchment paper.

7. Roll out the dough on a lightly floured surface till it's ½ inch thick.

8. Cut with a 2½-inch round cutter or a drinking glass. Line up on the baking sheets, at least 1 inch apart.

9. Bake for about 14 minutes or until lightly browned. Cool on baking sheets for 2 minutes. Remove to wire racks to cool completely.

The March Family

Party Tea

Louisa May Alcott's mother put this recipe for making tea in her little leather-covered book in 1856: "The proper way to make a cup of good tea, is a matter of some importance. The teapot is at once filled up with boiling water; then the tea is put into the pot, and is allowed to stand five minutes before it is used. The leaves gradually absorb the water, and as gradually sink to the bottom. The result is, that the tea leaves are not scalded, as they are when boiling water is poured over them, and you get all the true flavor of the tea. In truth, much less is required this way than under the old and common practice."[11]

11   Collins, *The Little Women Treasury*, 66.

Makes 4 servings

- 10 cups water
- 3 tablespoons loose tea leaves

1. Bring the water to a boil.

2. Pour 4 cups of boiling water into a large teapot, let it sit for 5 minutes, and then pour it out. (This step is called scalding the teapot.)

3. Pour another 4 cups boiling water into the teapot, and add tea leaves. Pour the remaining water into a smaller teapot so it's available for people who don't like strong tea to dilute their cup.

4. Let the tea steep—5 to 6 minutes for green tea, 10 to 12 for black tea—before pouring. (You can also try mixing half green and half black.)

Tidbit of History: Spilling the Tea

In 1773, anger over British taxes led to the Boston Tea Party, where demonstrators dumped 342 chests of tea into the harbor. During the American Revolution, it was considered unpatriotic to drink tea. After the war was over, America began trading directly with China (and later Japan), and tea slowly trickled back into the daily diet. By the 1860s, New York City boasted an impressive selection of tea shops. One of them, The Great American Tea Company, became the largest tea distributor in the country. (By the way, The Great American Tea Company eventually expanded its business, renamed itself A&P, and was the biggest grocery retailer in the U.S. for 60 years.)

The Great American Tea Company posted advertisements that listed their goods and prices in *Godey's Lady's Book*, one of the most popular 19th-century magazines. Some of their varieties are familiar to us, others not so much: For black teas, they offered Oolong and English Breakfast; for green, they had Imperial, Japan, Young Hyson, and the excitingly named Gunpowder.[12]

---

12   Louis A. Godey and Sarah J. Hale, *Godey's Lady's Book*, (Philadelphia: Louis A. Godey, 1867).

The March Family

Index

Further Reading

HISTORICAL COOKBOOKS CONSULTED

Our recipes were based on historical receipts from the following books:

Acton, Eliza. *Modern Cookery for Private Families.* London: Longmans, Green, Reader, and Dyer, 1868.

Alcott, Abba May. *Abigail May Alcott's Receipts & Simple Remedies.* Concord, MA: Nancy L. Kohl and the Louisa May Alcott Foundation, 1980.

Beauvilliers, A. B. *The Art of French Cookery.* London: Longman, Rees, Orme, Brown, and Green, 1827.

Beeton, Isabella. *Mrs Beeton's Book of Household Management.* London: S. O. Beeton, 1861.

Brisse, Léon. *Le calendrier gastronomique.* Paris: Bureaux de la Liberté, 1867.

Cardelli, P. and J.-S. Lionnet-Clémandot. *Nouveau manuel complet du confiseur et du chocolatier.* Paris: Librairie encyclopédique de Roret, 1862.

Carême, Marie-Antoine. *The Royal Parisian Pastrycook and Confectioner.* London: F. J. Mason, 1834.

Child, Lydia Maria. *The American Frugal Housewife.* Boston: Carter, Hendee, & Co., 1832.

Cornelius, Mary Hooker. *The Young Housekeeper's Friend.* Boston: Brown, Taggard, and Chase, 1859.

Dubois, Urbain. *Cuisine artistique: études de l'école moderne.* Paris: E. Dentu, 1872.

Dubois, Urbain, and Émile Bernard. *La cuisine classique.* Paris: E. Dentu, 1882.

Francatelli, Charles Elmé. *The Modern Cook.* London: Richard Bentley, 1846.

Francatelli, Charles Elmé. *The Royal English and Foreign Confectioner.* London: Chapman and Hall, 1862.

Hale, S. J. *The Good Housekeeper.* Boston: Weeks, Jordan, and Company, 1839.

Hall, Elizabeth M. *Practical American Cookery and Domestic Economy.* New York: C. M. Saxton, Barker & Co., 1860.

Knight S. G. *Tit-Bits: Or, How to Prepare a Nice Dish at a Moderate Expense.* Boston: Crosby and Nichols, 1864.

Leslie, Eliza. *Directions for Cookery, In Its Various Branches.* Philadelphia: Carey & Hart, 1840.

Leslie, Eliza. *Miss Leslie's Lady's New Receipt-Book.* Philadelphia: Carey & Hart, 1850.

Leslie, Eliza. *Seventy-Five Receipts for Pastry, Cakes, and Sweetmeats.* Boston: Munroe and Francis, 1828.

Viard, A. *Le cuisinier royal.* Paris: Gustave Barba, 1840.

Webster, A. L. *The Improved Housewife.* Boston: Phillips, Samson, and Company, 1855.

What Shall We Eat? A Manual for Housekeepers. New York: G. P. Putnam & Son, 1868.

WORKS CITED

If you'd like to know more fascinating historical details about Louisa May Alcott and life in 19th-century America, check out these sources:

Alcott, Louisa May. *Little Women: or, Meg, Jo, Beth, and Amy.* Boston: Little, Brown, and Company, 1896.

Dubois, Urbain. *Cuisine artistique: études de l'école moderne: Ouvrage en deux parties.* Paris: Librairie E. Dentu, 1872, 21–26.

Collins, Carolyn Strom, and Christina Wyss Eriksson. *Little Women Treasury.* New York: Viking Penguin, 1996.

Gamber, Wendy. *The Boardinghouse in Nineteenth-Century America.* Baltimore: Johns Hopkins University Press, 2007.

Godey, Louis A., and Sarah J. Hale. *Godey's Lady's Book.* Philadelphia: Louis A. Godey, 1867.

Veit, Helen Zoe. *Food in the Civil War Era: The North.* East Lansing: Michigan State University Press, 2014.

Ziedrich, Linda. *The Joy of Pickling.* Quarto Publishing Group, 201), 100

OUR BLOG

Visit our blog, 36eggs.com, for extra recipes, more background information, and our detailed timeline of the *Little Women* novel, as well as lists of all the food and beverages that are mentioned in the story!

Acknowledgments

As librarians, we are obviously big fans of books, but we never expected to write one ourselves. And because we're newbie authors, it took the support of a whole village of friends, family, and kind strangers to complete this project, which is very dear to our hearts.

First, we would be remiss if we didn't thank our editor and publisher, Casie Vogel and Ulysses Press, for entrusting this book to us—it has been a great honor as well as a joy to work on. We are grateful too, to Lilly Ghahremani, our literary agent, for her invaluable guidance.

We would like to recognize the librarians, historians, and researchers who generously responded with enthusiasm and expertise when we contacted them out of the blue for advice: Michael Krondl, Helen Zoe Veit, Leslie Wilson, Erica J. Peters, Megan Elias, Valérie Dugas, Valérie Ammirati, Véronique Jira, and Loïc Bienassis.

We are also very grateful to our friends who helped us with the writing process. Their assistance included but was not limited to: searching for resources; editing, testing, and tasting recipes (even the weird ones); consulting as fellow fans of the novel, trying the many iterations of the personality quiz; and translating messages and information between English and French. Thank you to Beston Barnett, Erik Bergstrom, Vicki Bergstrom, Haley Bochler, Sara Nielsen, Susan del Castillo, Molly Fischer, Declan Fleming, Jenn Frohlich, Janet Gastil, Sarah Hiller-Venegas, Michael Ho, Hildie Kraus, Jennifer Lawson, Katherine Matlack, Matt Meola, Hannah O'Neill, Chisato Osada, Sarah Parylak, Lessa Pelayo-Lozada, Erin Pitts, Ramona Price, Phil Shopoff, Laurie Stein, Liz Vagani, Howie Wang, Alli Wilson, Nick Wilson, Laura Yamaguchi, and especially Whitney McBride-Carlson and Jamie Wilger.

About the Authors

JENNE BERGSTROM was raised by two summer camp directors but spent all her time reading instead of going outdoors. She went to a tiny one-room schoolhouse in a charming mountain town but always dreamed of living in a glamorous big city. Nowadays, she lives in a tiny house in San Diego, and supervises both urban and rural libraries. She is the cofounder of the literary culinary blog 36eggs.com, and her favorite *Little Women* character is Aunt March.

MIKO OSADA is a librarian for kids and teens, in a suburb just east of San Diego. She lives with her wife and their two cats, Squeazle and Baby. Miko is the cocreator of 36eggs.com, a blog about re-creating fictitious dishes. *Little Women* was one of her favorite stories growing up, and she owns four copies of the book: two in Japanese (her first language) and two in English. The March sister she relates to most is Amy.